THE WAITING ROOM

BY LISA LOOMER

★

★

DRAMATISTS
PLAY SERVICE
INC.

THE WAITING ROOM
Copyright © 1998, Lisa Loomer

SPECIAL NOTE

World Premiere produced by Center Theatre Group/
Mark Taper Forum of Los Angeles
Gordon Davidson, Artistic Director/Producer

THE WAITING ROOM received its New York premiere at the
Vineyard Theatre, New York.

SPECIAL NOTE ON SONGS AND RECORDINGS

To Mimi Loomer

THE WAITING ROOM was produced by the Vineyard Theatre (Douglas Aibel, Artistic Director) in New York City, in November 1996. It was directed by David Schweizer; the set design was by G.W. Mercier; the costume design was by Gail Brassard; the lighting design was by Peter Kaczorowski; the sound design was by Darron L. West; the original music was composed by Mitchell Greenhill; and the production stage manager was Elizabeth M. Berther. The cast was as follows:

VICTORIA	Veanne Cox
FORGIVENESS FROM HEAVEN	June Kyoko Lu
WANDA	Chloe Webb
DOUGLAS	Byron Jennings
LARRY	Damian Young
KEN	Lou Liberatore
OLIVER	William Langan
BLESSING FROM HEAVEN	James Saito
BRENDA, OTHERS	Michelle Shay
ORDERLIES	Dylan Grewan, Mike Toto

THE WAITING ROOM was produced in conjunction with the Mark Taper Forum (Gordon Davidson, Artistic Director; Charles Dillingham, Managing Director) at Arena Stage (Douglas C. Wager, Artistic Director; Kyle Donnelly, Producing Director) in Washington, D.C., on December 8, 1995. It was directed by David Schweizer; the set design was by James Youmans; the costume design was by David Woolard; the lighting design was by Nancy Schertler; the sound design was by Jon Gottlieb and Mitchell Greenhill; the original music was by Mitchell Greenhill; and the stage manager was Robert Witherow. The cast was as follows:

FORGIVENESS FROM HEAVEN .... June Kyoko Lu
VICTORIA .... Pamela Nyberg
BRENDA, BRIDGET, JADE ORNAMENT, CERISE,
NURSE BRUCE, JAMAICAN WAITRESS .... Leah Maddrie
WANDA .... Linda Gehringer
DOUGLAS .... John Bennett Perry
OLIVER.. Henry Strozier
KEN .... David Marks
LARRY .... Tim Monsion
BLESSING FROM HEAVEN .... James Saito
ORDERLIES .... Bill Delaney, David M. Fendig,
Michael J. Swaine

THE WAITING ROOM was produced by Trinity Repertory Company (Oskar Eustis, Artistic Director; Patricia Egan, Managing Director) in Providence, Rhode Island, on October 25, 1994. It was directed by David Schweizer; the set design was by Michael McGarty; the costume design was by William Lane; the lighting design was by Russell Champa; the sound design was by Jon Gottlieb and Mitchell Greenhill; the original music was by Mitchell Greenhill; the dramaturg was Tori Haring-Smith; and the stage manager was Thomas M. Kauffman. The cast was as follows:

FORGIVENESS FROM HEAVEN .... June Kyoko Lu
VICTORIA.. Anne Scurria
BRENDA, BRIDGET, JADE ORNAMENT, CERISE,
NURSE BRUCE, JAMAICAN WAITRESS .... Rose Weaver
WANDA... Janice Duclos
DOUGLAS .... William Damkoehler
OLIVER.. Ed Shea
KEN... Stephen Berenson
LARRY .... Dan Welch
BLESSING FROM HEAVEN...................................... Chil Kong
ORDERLIES .... Gabriel Diamond, Robert Grady

THE WAITING ROOM received its world premiere at the Mark Taper Forum (Gordon Davidson, Artistic Director; Charles Dillingham, Managing Director) in Los Angeles, California, on July 31, 1994. It was directed by David Schweizer; the set design was by Mark Wendland; the costume design was by Deborah Nadoolman; the lighting design was by Anne Militello; the sound design was by Jon Gottlieb and Mitchell Greenhill; the original music was by Mitchell Greenhill; and the production stage manager was Mary Michele Miner. The cast was as follows:

FORGIVENESS FROM HEAVEN .... June Kyoko Lu
VICTORIA .... Lela Ivey
BRENDA, BRIDGET, JADE ORNAMENT, CERISE,
NURSE BRUCE, JAMAICAN WAITRESS .... Leah Maddrie
WANDA.. Jacalyn O'Shaughnessy
DOUGLAS.. Robert Picardo
OLIVER .... Simon Templeman
KEN .... Tony Simotes
LARRY... Kurt Fuller
BLESSING FROM HEAVEN .... Jim Ishida
ORDERLIES................. Brian Brophy, Ken Narasaki, Jason Reed

THE WAITING ROOM received a workshop production at Williamstown Theatre Festival (Peter Hunt, Artistic Director; William Stewart, Managing Director) in Williamstown, Massachusetts, on July 28, 1993. It was directed by David Schweizer; the set design was by Douglas Huszti; the costume design was by Jeanette DeJong; the lighting design was by Betsy Finston; the original sound design and music were by Mitchell Greenhill; the sound design was by Matthew Bennett; and the stage manager was Tara M. Galvin. The cast was as follows:

VICTORIA	Jessica Hendra
FORGIVENESS FROM HEAVEN	June Kyoko Lu
WANDA	Jacalyn O'Shaughnessy
DOUGLAS	Victor Slezak
LARRY	Kurt Fuller
KEN	Tony Simotes
OLIVER	James Matthew Ryan
BLESSING FROM HEAVEN	James Saito
BRENDA, BRIDGET, JADE ORNAMENT, CERISE, NURSE BRUCE, ETC.	Leah Maddrie
ORDERLIES	Evan Alexander Robertson; Brian Hutchinson

CHARACTERS

VICTORIA — A tightly corseted English Victorian woman, early thirties. Curious, intelligent, and wily. Strong opinions and excellent manners cover considerable panic, confusion, and wonder.

FORGIVENESS FROM HEAVEN — A wealthy eighteenth-century Chinese woman with bound feet. Late forties, sensual and dutiful, with an enduring smile.

WANDA — A modern gal from Jersey. Forty. Enormous breasts and perfected everything else, too. Ballsy, great laugh, but as vulnerable as she appears streetwise, and smarter than she's gone out of her way to look.

DOUGLAS — A surgeon. Forties. Excellent with bodies, and befuddled by the people who inhabit them. Funny in the way he always misses the joke. A principled, earnest, driven, and awfully decent man, in an impossible situation. Not that he doesn't care, he's just got a full waiting room.

LARRY — A vice president of a major drug company. Also on the board of a major cancer center. A big charmer, but an even better businessman. Disarming and utterly convincing.

KEN — An official of the FDA. A scientist turned bureaucrat. Trying to do a good job but dying to be liked.

OLIVER — A Victorian doctor. Decorous and jolly, with a tightly buttoned dark side.

BLESSING FROM HEAVEN — An eighteenth-century Chinese businessman. A loving husband, with too many wives. Sexy. But above all, proud.

BRENDA — A Jamaican nurse in her thirties. Bright, no-nonsense, with the keen insight and irony of the outsider. Moves easily from "proper" speech to patois. The actress who plays her also plays the following six other characters, and is, as Brenda, the keeper of their humor, wisdom, and rage.

BRIDGET — A paranoid, pregnant Irish maid.

JADE ORNAMENT — A young, impressionable Chinese maid.

A PUERTO RICAN HEALTH CLUB ATTENDANT

AN AFRO-AMERICAN MASSEUSE

CERISE — A sassy French secretary. Extravagantly flirtatious.

NURSE BRUCE — A gay African-American nurse. Been there, done that.

JOHNNY — A friendly bartender, played by the actor who plays Blessing.

INTERN — Played by the actor who plays Blessing.

ASIAN MASSEUSE — Played by the actress who plays Forgiveness.

WOMAN LAWYER — HATES MEN! Played by the actress who plays Victoria.

MALE LAWYER — Played by the actor who plays Oliver.

ASIAN CABBIE — Played by the actress who plays Forgiveness.

TIME

The past, and the present, and often both at once.

PLACE

New York City, England, and China.

SOME NOTES ON PRODUCTION

The set should be flexible, humorous, and not too literal, as if for a modern fairy tale. If hospital images are used, it is important that the overall look not be cold.

The play benefits from moving as quickly and simply as possible from scene to scene. If transitions are seen, they can be thought of as bleeds, moments for characters to pass through each other's lives as they set props, or move into or out of a scene. But they should not "comment" on the play, change the tone, or slow it down. Along with the actors, two stagehands, as Orderlies, can assist with changes.

Music enhances the mix of worlds in this play, from ancient Chinese music to Prince.* Wanda, Forgiveness, and Victoria should each have a musical theme.

In terms of Brenda's dialect, phrases like "chu," "hmmnn-hmmnn" and "eeh hee" are intended to have the Jamaican, not the American, sound.

The tone of the play sits on the edge of funny and dead serious. If the playing style is *slightly* stylized as opposed to "naturalistic," the emotions are still completely true. Please avoid caricature, trusting that all of these characters are doing the best they can, given the values of their cultures and the constraints of their times.

* See Special Note on Songs and Recordings on copyright page.

THE WAITING ROOM

ACT ONE

Scene 1

The Waiting Room. Three chairs and a table with magazines. Boppy elevator music, possibly a Beatles* tune.

Victoria, dressed in twenty pounds of clothes and tightly corseted, and Forgiveness From Heaven, in ancient Chinese robes ... wait. After several moments of waiting, Forgiveness picks up Vogue. *She sniffs a perfume ad, delighted. Victoria picks up* Cosmopolitan, *is horrified by the cover, and quickly puts it down. Finally, she takes a book from under her skirt and begins to read.*

FORGIVENESS. Pretty. Pretty, pretty ... *(Shows Victoria the magazine.)* Pretty, huh?
VICTORIA. *(Politely.)* Yes. *(She goes back to her book.)*
FORGIVENESS. *(Eager to chat.)* Long wait, huh?
VICTORIA. He's thorough. *(A bloodcurdling scream offstage. The women barely react.)*
FORGIVENESS. Good doctor.
VICTORIA. Oh yes. *(Forgiveness smiles. Victoria remembers her manners and holds out her hand.)* Ah — Victoria Smoot.
FORGIVENESS. Forgiveness From Heaven. *(Forgiveness doesn't know what to do with Victoria's extended hand. She gives it a little tap.)*
VICTORIA. How do you do. *(She starts to go back to her book.)*
FORGIVENESS. Oh, fine. *(Smiles.)* Little problem with little toe.
VICTORIA. Well, I'm sure the doctor will fix it.
FORGIVENESS. Fell off this morning.

---

* See Special Note on Songs and Recordings on copyright page.

13

VICTORIA. I'm so sorry. And your family? Your husband is well?

FORGIVENESS. *(Smiles, covering pain.)* With other wives this week.

VICTORIA. Nice for you … *(Sniffs.)* By the way, do you smell something — untoward?

FORGIVENESS. *(Proudly.)* My feet!

VICTORIA. I beg your pardon?

FORGIVENESS. My feet. Stink bad, huh?

VICTORIA. No, no, not — *too* awfully.

FORGIVENESS. I would wash them, but my husband, he's crazy for the smell. Likes to eat watermelon seeds from the toes. Almonds. *(Delighted.)* Dirt.

VICTORIA. Well … *(What can she say?)* I *love* your shoes. *(She starts to go back to her book.)*

FORGIVENESS. Size three.

VICTORIA. Three *inches*?!

FORGIVENESS. *(Competitive.)* What size your waist?

VICTORIA. Sixteen. I got my first corset quite young.

FORGIVENESS. How young?

VICTORIA. Fourteen!

FORGIVENESS. *(Tops her; shows feet.)* I was five. *(Almost hopeful.)* Corset hurts bad, huh?

VICTORIA. Oh, no. Only when I breathe.

FORGIVENESS. My feet, just first couple years.

VICTORIA. Really?

FORGIVENESS. My mother, you see —

VICTORIA. *(Reflexively polite.)* How is she?

FORGIVENESS. Oh, dead long time now.

VICTORIA. Nice for her …

FORGIVENESS. One day mother say to me, "Forgiveness From Heaven, today is lucky day by the moon. Time to start binding … "

VICTORIA. Ah.

FORGIVENESS. *(Like a recipe.)* Then mother takes bandage, place on inside of instep, and carry over small toes to force them in and towards the sole. Then bandage is wrapped around heel nice and forcefully, so heel and toes are drawn close, real close together.

VICTORIA. I see. *(It slips out.)* Why?

FORGIVENESS. Make feet pretty for future husband! *(Laughs.)* That night, I tried to run away in the forest — my feet were on fire! But mother found me and forced me to walk. She was a good girl when her feet were bound and never cried.

14

VICTORIA. *(Sighs.)* And so your poor feet never grew.

FORGIVENESS. *(Recounts her ordeal with a cheeriness bordering on relish.)* Got smaller! Soon the flesh became putrescent, and little pieces sloughed off from the sole as toes began to putrefy. *(Laughs.)* When I ate salted fish, my feet would swell and pus would drip — oh terrible! *(This is making Victoria rather ill.)* Mother would remove bindings, lance corns with a needle, and wipe the pus and blood and dead flesh ... And every two weeks I changed shoes, each pair one-quarter-inch smaller. *(Victoria starts to gag and gets out her smelling salts.)* And after two years, my feet were practically dead — so no more pain! Finally, all the bones were broken and four toes bent in nice neat row towards plantar. *(Victoria falls back in her chair, faint. Forgiveness concludes, triumphantly.)* And when I was nine ... father betrothed me to my husband!

VICTORIA. Well. *(Pause.)* I love your shoes. *(A scream offstage.)*

FORGIVENESS. And what are *you* being treated for?

VICTORIA. Me? Oh ... *(Yawns.)* Hysteria.

FORGIVENESS. Hys — teria?

VICTORIA. It's a disease of the ovaries.

FORGIVENESS. Hurts bad, huh?

VICTORIA. *(Condescending.)* No, no, no. You see, the ovaries control the personality. I've done some reading on the matter. Though my husband says that reading makes me worse. Romantic novels especially. *(Proud.)* My husband is a doctor. *(Victoria has a tic. Whenever she says the word "husband," her lower arm flings out from the waist, as if to swat someone.)*

FORGIVENESS. Lucky. He has treated you?

VICTORIA. Well, he did prescribe the rest cure.

FORGIVENESS. Nice and peaceful?

VICTORIA. *(Like Forgiveness, Victoria too tries to put a good spin on things.)* Oh very. Six weeks on one's back in a dimly lit room. No reading, no visitors, no ... potty.

FORGIVENESS. Worked good?

VICTORIA. Well, I came out screaming, actually. But it was hardly my husband's fault. It seems — well, it seems I've had too much education and my uterus has atrophied commensurately.

FORGIVENESS. Glad I never went to school.

VICTORIA. Lucky.

FORGIVENESS. When I was a little girl, my husband liked my little feet so much, I never left the bedroom.

VICTORIA. Well, children need rest.

FORGIVENESS. Men crazy for the golden lotus. Feel much love and pity for your suffering ... *(She gets up and demonstrates.)* The tiny steps, the whispered walk ... *(Makes a circle.)* And bound feet make buttocks larger, more attractive.

VICTORIA. Well, I assure you, it's a lot less fuss to wear a bustle —

FORGIVENESS. Bustle? Not natural! Also, foot binding makes vagina tighter. *(Victoria has another tic: sex makes her nose twitch.)* When I walk, whole lower part of my body is in state of tension, so vagina becomes like little fist!

VICTORIA. *(After a beat.)* Mrs. From Heaven, you do know erotic tendencies are one of the primary symptoms of ovarian disease —

FORGIVENESS. *(Worried.)* Erotic tendencies are symptom of disease?

VICTORIA. Obviously you do not keep abreast of modern science.

FORGIVENESS. But what if husband *insists* on erotic tendencies?

VICTORIA. Well, that's not your "tendency," dear, that's your *duty. (Leans in.)* And need we mention the perils of the ah ... well, the, ah ... vice?

FORGIVENESS. The vice?

VICTORIA. Leads to lesions, TB, dementia — I strap the children's hands down every night! *(A scream offstage.)* And catch it early because clitorectomy and cauterization can be quite costly. *(Brenda enters with clipboard.)*

BRENDA. Which one of you ladies was here first?

VICTORIA and FORGIVENESS. *(Pointing.)* She was!

BRENDA. The doctor will be right with you. *(She exits.)*

FORGIVENESS. *(Scared.)* This — vice — can cause disease in grown women too?

VICTORIA. Mrs. From Heaven. There are even *some* women who become enthralled by the stimulation of gynecological instruments! *(Twitching.)* — begging every doctor to institute an examination of the, ah — the ah, sexual ah —

FORGIVENESS. Wait just minute, Mrs. Smoot. *(Defensive; huffy.)* I'm only here to have toe put back! Only here for that reason!

VICTORIA. *(Huffier.)* Well! I'm just here to see about removing the ovaries! *(Wanda enters in an outfit which pays homage to her enormous breasts. She carries a backbreaking pocketbook and a clipboard with her chart, and takes the empty seat between them.)*

WANDA. Excuse me, you reading that *Cosmo?*

VICTORIA. Take it!

FORGIVENESS. *Both* ovaries? *(As Victoria speaks, Wanda is distracted by her story.)*

VICTORIA. *(With mounting hysteria.)* Well, we've tried everything else! Injections to the womb — water, milk, tea, a decoction of marshmallow. I've stopped reading and writing, stopped stimulating my emotions with operas and French plays. Last week the doctor placed leeches on my *vulva* — *(Wanda's mouth falls open. She gets out her cigarettes.)* Some were quite adventurous, actually, and traveled all the way to the cervical cavity! The pressure from the corset's forcing my uterus out through my vagina … And according to my husband, my hysteria's only getting worse! My husband says I've all the classic symptoms of ovarian disease: troublesomeness, eating like a ploughman, painful menstruation — a desire to learn *Greek*! Attempted suicide, persecution mania, and simple cussedness! Last night I sneezed continuously for twenty-seven minutes, and tried to *bite* my own husband! What can I do?! I shan't be beaten across the face and body with wet towels like an Irish woman — I JUST WANT THE DAMN THINGS OUT!

WANDA. *(After a beat.)* Just the way I feel about my tits. *(Quick freeze on the three of them looking out with their concerns. Then, in the transition to the next scene, Wanda's theme music comes up as she get ready for her exam.)*

Scene 2

The examining room. An examining bed, screen, and chair.

Wanda, in a white paper gown, is giving information to Brenda, who's on the fine line between brusqueness and dis-approval. Wanda's trying to get Brenda to like her.

BRENDA. Name?

WANDA. *(Loves it.)* Wanda. *(Hates it.)* Kozynski.

BRENDA. Date of birth?

WANDA. *(Smiles.)* I'm thirty-five.

BRENDA. Date of birth?

WANDA. *(Figuring it out.)* Uh … nineteen-fifty — *(Seamlessly.)* sixty-one. *(Smiles; sure.)* June twenty-first.

BRENDA. Place of birth?

WANDA. *(Proudly.)* New York.

BRENDA. *(Suspicious.)* What part of New York, Ms. Kozynski?

WANDA. Jersey. Hey, I'm sorry I forgot to fill out my forms. A couple of the gals and I started to chat and … can I get an "Incomplete"?

BRENDA. *(Dryly.)* No problem. Do you have insurance?

WANDA. I just started a new job. It hasn't kicked in yet. The insurance.

BRENDA. Do you smoke?

WANDA. *(Takes pack from purse.)* Want one?

BRENDA. Birth control pills?

WANDA. Not on me —

BRENDA. *(Gives her a look and continues writing.)* Any operations? Surgical procedures?

WANDA. No.

BRENDA. Not even for … cosmetic purposes?

WANDA. *(Laughs.)* Oh. Well, I had my nose done. *(Beat.)* And they left too much cartilage, so I had to do it again. *(Beat.)* And then I had to have the chin enhancement to match. *(Beat.)* And cheekbones. Uh … lipo — tummy and thighs … *(Brenda struggles to write it all down.)* No arms. Just tummy and —

BRENDA. Thighs. I got it. *(Stares at Wanda's chest.)* Anything else?

WANDA. *(Laughs.)* Well — my tits.

BRENDA. *(She likes Wanda less and less.)* And when was that?

WANDA. I got them for my thirty — *(Catches herself.)* eth birthday. They were a present. From my father. Okay, so … *(Counts on breasts.)* Tits in, tits out … new tits in … new tits out … plus the tits I have now —

BRENDA. *(Trying to follow.)* So that's three tit — breasts?

WANDA. Three *sets*. Six tits. *(Laughs.)* They always get the math right. And nobody ever called me "Pancake" again. You got a nickname? "Cookie" or something?

BRENDA. No. Have you experienced problems with your implants, Ms. Kozynski?

WANDA. Oh, the usual. The foam broke down. The casing hardened. It's funny, I can keep a couch six years, I can't keep a pair of tits six months. And it's not like anybody's jumpin' up and down on 'em, if you know what I mean. Not that I'd feel a damn thing if they did. My *Hyundai* should be this solid. *(Punches chest.)* Wanna take a punch?

BRENDA. *(Hard.)* Any other operations?

WANDA. *(Hard.)* Yeah. Tonsillectomy.

BRENDA. The doctor will be right with you. *(She leaves. The doctor, Douglas, rolls onstage, already in his chair, his nose in her chart. His greeting is perfunctory, doctor-cheery.)*

DOUGLAS. Good morning.

WANDA. Absolutely.

DOUGLAS. *(Reading.)* Well, let's see what we have here. Hmmmn ... *(Rises.)* Lie down please, and just open your gown so I have access ... *(He goes behind the screen and washes his hands.)*

WANDA. Okay — *(Douglas peeks out and looks at her for the first time, noting the breasts.)*

DOUGLAS. *(What can he say?)* Oh. Fine. *(He goes to Wanda and begins to manipulate the mammaries.)* Uh-huh ... Uh-huh ... Very good ... Just lift your arms over your head, please. That's fine. Good. And let's see now ... *(Hoists implant.)* Uh-huh — *(The intercom rings.)*

VOICE ON INTERCOM. Dr. McCaskill, Mrs. Peterson, line one.

DOUGLAS. Excuse me. *(He picks up the phone. Doctor-cheery.)* Hello? ... That's perfectly normal, Mrs. Peterson ... It's perfectly normal ... No, it's normal ... Call me if it turns green. Bye-bye. *(He goes back to Wanda, picking up where he left off, trying to get around those implants. Hoisting with great effort.)* Mmmn-hmmn. Mmmn-hmmm. You can relax your arms now. *(Clears throat.)* All right. Fine. *(He goes back to his chair and reads Wanda's chart. Wanda sits up. He clears his throat again. Without looking up.)* That's it, you can sit up now. *(Wanda clears her throat. He looks up.)* Oh. Have you noticed any change in your breasts, Ms. ... *(Checks chart; mispronounces.)* Koz ... nicki? You haven't mentioned experiencing any pain.

WANDA. Only when I watch TV.

DOUGLAS. When you — ?

WANDA. You know, all those talk shows. "I Got Scleriowhatsis From My Implants," and Geraldo had on this transsexual typist who got rheumatoid arthritis and couldn't type — I'm a secretary, doc, I gotta type. Hey, a gal in our office got a razor and took hers out herself —

DOUGLAS. No, no, we can certainly do that for you. If that's what you decide.

WANDA. *(Flirtatious.)* What do *you* think?

DOUGLAS. Well, the FDA believes there is not enough evidence to justify having silicone implants removed if the woman is not having symptoms.

WANDA. *(Pats chest.)* Good!

DOUGLAS. Unfortunately, there is no sure way to monitor for bleed, leakage, rupture —

WANDA. What would you advise your daughter?

DOUGLAS. *(Bewildered.)* I don't have a daughter —

WANDA. But if you did.

DOUGLAS. *(Looks at breasts.)* And she had, uh …

WANDA. Yeah.

DOUGLAS. Well … *(Thinks.)* I'd have to speak with her doctor. *(Back to her chart.)* Any cancer in your family, Ms. … *(Shakes head.)* Koz — niskaya?

WANDA. Uh … *(Pause.)* Sure. My grandmother on my father's side … my grandfather on my mother's side. My mother's sister … and brother. His wife —

DOUGLAS. Just blood relations, please.

WANDA. Oh. Okay. And my mother and father.

DOUGLAS. *(Writing.)* That's it?

WANDA. Well, I had an uncle who had it in the prostate. But he didn't die from it.

DOUGLAS. *(Writing.)* That's good.

WANDA. He died in Atlantic City. Ever been there?

DOUGLAS. No, can't say I have.

WANDA. He died right on the boardwalk. *(Beat.)* With an icepick in his head. He was lucky — *(She bursts out laughing. Douglas looks at her, confused. She lets it go.)*

DOUGLAS. Ever have a mammogram?

WANDA. *(Flirting.)* I'm only thirty-five.

DOUGLAS. Well, I'm going to send you for one.

WANDA. I had one last year.

DOUGLAS. Oh good. *(Rises.)* I'll have my nurse phone your previous physician and then we can compare.

WANDA. Nurses?

DOUGLAS. I'm sorry — ? *(Wanda shakes her head, "never mind." He wheels over to the door, then stops and asks … Concerned.)* By the way, did the doctor who gave you those implants ask you any questions?

WANDA. Yeah. *(Smiles.)* "What size?" *(Douglas nods and wheels out.)*

Scene 3

A Victorian bedroom. A screen, a well-dressed bed. Oliver's smoking jacket hangs on a medical mannequin.

Victoria is in bed, reading voraciously. There's a knock at the door. Victoria quickly hides her book under the mattress.

VICTORIA. *(Brightly.)* Come in! *(Bridget, the maid, enters with a duster — the only weapon she's got. The encounter is a duet of suspicion and paranoia, a dance for power.)*
BRIDGET. *(Curtsies.)* Shall I straighten, ma'am?
VICTORIA. Please. *(Bridget begins to dust the mannequin with a fury. Carefully.)* Bridget ...
BRIDGET. Ma'am?
VICTORIA. While you were making up the bed this morning ... did you happen to pick up ... under the mattress, say —
BRIDGET. Don't go under the mattress! *(Darkly.)* Why would I? *(She starts dusting around Victoria, nearly dusting her off the bed.)*
VICTORIA. Well, I don't know, Bridget ... to ah, clean under it I suppose. And perhaps, by chance, in the course of your cleaning, you might have happened to find —
BRIDGET. *(A dare.)* Found what ma'am? What might I have found? *(She plumps the pillows fiercely, giving one a good punch.)*
VICTORIA. Well ... If you *do* happen to find something Bridget ... Don't trouble my husband with it — just bring it to me.
BRIDGET. Very good, ma'am. I'll do just that. *(Beat; cagey.)* 'Cept how will I recognize it ma'am? Bein' as I've never seen it before?
VICTORIA. Oh. *(Hesitantly.)* Well, it looks rather like a ... a ... a book, Bridget.
BRIDGET. *(She busts out laughing.)* A book, ma'am? It's a book?!
OLIVER. *(Offstage sing-song.)* Swee-tums! *(Both women panic.)*
VICTORIA. Shut up. *(Quickly.)* I mean — open the drapes.
BRIDGET. *(Scared.)* The drapes?

VICTORIA. Open them, Bridget. And see the girls are washed and combed for supper. And no bird in Felicity's bonnet! *(The dance begins again.)*

BRIDGET. *(Paranoid.)* I didn't put no bird! Where would I get a bird?

VICTORIA. Where indeed, Bridget. Where indeed. *(Oliver enters in excellent good cheer.)*

OLIVER. Home ... home ... home! Bridget — are you putting on weight? *(Bridget shakes her head, "no!" Jolly.)* Very good then! *(Bridget curtsies and runs.)*

VICTORIA. How are you, Oliver?

OLIVER. Very well, my love. I had an excellent lunch, a rather tedious amputation, and I'm pleased to return to this vestal temple of cheerfulness and repose — *(Kisses her hand.)* and to you. You visited the doctor?

VICTORIA. Of course.

OLIVER. *(Feeling Victoria's forehead.)* Were you there long, sweetums?

VICTORIA. *(Painstakingly careful with her husband.)* Till two-seventeen. *(Lies.)* You see, the doctor was called away on an emergency, Oliver —

OLIVER. *(Concerned.)* I see. So you — ? *(He starts to change into his smoking jacket.)*

VICTORIA. I had tea with a lady named Wanda. Who was also waiting.

OLIVER. For, love?

VICTORIA. An examination of the breasts.

OLIVER. *(Lascivious chuckle.)* I see ...

VICTORIA. Oliver ... She mentioned the work of a doctor who has had some excellent results — without surgery — in cases such as my own. *(Oliver starts to look for his cigars.)*

OLIVER. And whom did the lady with the breasts mention?

VICTORIA. A Dr. Freud.

OLIVER. *(Looking around.)* Freud ...

VICTORIA. He seems to feel that hysteria can be treated, not by operating on the ovaries, but rather by treating the —

OLIVER. *(Finds cigars.)* Ah!

VICTORIA. Mind. *(Oliver lights up and puffs away.)*

OLIVER. *(Pleasantly.)* Dr. Freud theorizes, love, that hysteria is a reaction to repressed desires for incestuous relations with a parent

22

of the opposite sex. *(Victoria tries to form words; can't. Pleasantly curious.)* Were you attracted sexually to your father? *(Victoria sneezes.)* And did you feel an urge to kill your mother in order to facilitate the consummation of sexual relations with your father?

VICTORIA. I adored my mother!

OLIVER. Charming woman, I adored her myself. Perhaps, indeed, somewhat more even than my own dear — *(He has a tic or stammer on his —)* mother. So you adored your mother ... But you *desired* your father?

VICTORIA. *(Confused.)* No, no, no! I didn't even like my father. I mean — I loved my father, of course. As one would love a — well — a father! He was a fine man — and an extraordinary physician.

OLIVER. But you didn't want to sleep with him?

VICTORIA. Oliver, I swear, I've never wanted to sleep with *any* man!

OLIVER. *(Beat; jolly.)* Jolly good then! I don't see that a visit to Dr. Freud will be of much use. On the contrary, it seems the mere discussion of his theories has upset you terribly.

VICTORIA. *(Upset.)* I'm not upset. *(Oliver touches her cheeks and is aroused by their warmth despite himself.)*

OLIVER. Your cheeks are flushed, and you're looking quite animated —

VICTORIA. I'm perfectly calm, Oliver. I just wondered if there were not one more course to try before removing the —

OLIVER. Now sweetums, we've had the most excellent results in cases such as your own. The moral sense is elevated, the woman becomes calm, industrious, cleanly —

VICTORIA. I *am* cleanly! *(She coughs from the cigar.)*

OLIVER. *(Aroused.)* Your hair is loose and the bedclothes are all in a dither —

VICTORIA. Oliver —

OLIVER. *(Truly pained.)* Can I bear to see your hopes raised and dashed yet another time? Not to mention the cost —

VICTORIA. *(Indignant.)* I'm sorry to be such a burden to you!

OLIVER. *(Wounded.)* How can you?

VICTORIA. I'm sorry.

OLIVER. I was going to say the cost to your children. Weeks and months away from them in hospitals, at rest cures and spas — like my own — *(Tic or stammer.)* mother, gadding about the continent ...

VICTORIA. I'm sorry, Oliver. I was just reading — *(Quickly.)* glancing — at the work of this Freud, and —

OLIVER. Again, love? You have read something and it has upset you. *(Sighs.)* Perhaps you simply do not want to get well. Perhaps it is, in fact, easier to lie on your pillows and let your children be raised by an Irishwoman, as did my own — *(Worse tic or stammer.)* mother, with her charities and basset hounds —

VICTORIA. Oliver!

OLIVER. And let your husband go to parties on his own —

VICTORIA. Listen to me!

OLIVER. *(Emotional.)* You're getting hysterical. *(Checks watch; pleasantly.)* Shall we have supper?

VICTORIA. LISTEN TO ME!

OLIVER. I'm due at the hospital —

VICTORIA. *(Drumming her legs.)* Grrrrrr!

OLIVER. So much for a peaceful supper.

VICTORIA. *(Bursts into tears.)* Oliver — I am afraid. *(Oliver rushes to her and holds her.)*

OLIVER. *(Moved.)* My sweetest girl, do you think I would let anything in the wide world harm you? Lie down, sweet. Lie down. There. I'll draw the drapes. *(He does.)* The air is exciting you. There now. Just rest. *(As he tucks her in, her arm flings out, hitting him.)* Oh, I say —

VICTORIA. Sorry — *(Her arm flings out three times, exciting him.)*

OLIVER. Vixen!

VICTORIA. I'm sorry — I'm sorry — *(Oliver must hold her down.)*

OLIVER. *(Aroused; guilty.)* Please, Victoria — not — not again, love —

VICTORIA. NO! *(She bites him.)*

OLIVER. No biting, love! *(Victoria kicks. He tries to restrain her.)* Now, now — no kicking. Please, Viccums — you know I — *(Husky.)* I'm sorry. I'm sorry, love — *(Suddenly he finds himself pulling the comforter down, and her nightgown up.)*

VICTORIA. Oliver — ! *(Oliver whips open his pants.)*

OLIVER. I love you. I love you, love. *(Mounts her.)* I love you, sweetums. Oh! Oh! *(Finishes, sighs.)* Oh. *(A pause. Then a loud sneeze from Victoria.)*

Scene 4

A golf course. Douglas prepares for his shot with a surgeon's precision … but fails.

DOUGLAS. GODDAMMIT! Fucking shit — piss … Darn. *(His companion, Oliver, enters with antique clubs, and prepares for his turn. He gets the ball in the hole and is quite pleased with himself. Douglas mutters "shit," then:)* Nice drive.

OLIVER. My dear fellow — trying day?

DOUGLAS. Double mastectomy, hysterectomy … and then I had to treat a toe.

OLIVER. A toe?

DOUGLAS. Chinese woman. Foot binding. I cannot describe to you the smell.

OLIVER. Barbaric. Utterly. *(They move to another area.)* By the way, I do hate to impose, but can you possibly fit my wife in this week?

DOUGLAS. *(Wary.)* For?

OLIVER. Ovariotomy?

DOUGLAS. Well, I'd like to accommodate you, Oliver, but I *will* have to examine her again. And last week she just jumped off the table and ran out of the office. Oliver — she bit my nurse.

OLIVER. Your *nurse*? Good grief. *(Shocked.)* She never bites strangers. It is a conundrum … obviously, the hysteria is only getting worse. The poor child is talking about Freud now, wondering if the problem in her ovaries might be cured via the mind.

DOUGLAS. Tell me about it. I have patients who come in, say they're going to beat *cancer* by visualizing armies of white cells with little bayonets charging through their bloodstream. *(He makes another lousy shot.)* GODDAMMIT!

OLIVER. Do tell.

DOUGLAS. One woman comes in, nods like golf balls, what does she want?

OLIVER. French comedies?

DOUGLAS. A hug. *(Oliver prepares for his shot.)*

OLIVER. A hug? Disgusting.

DOUGLAS. No, no, she's reading a book. A doctor! A surgeon! Advocates hugs. For the immune system. *(Ken and Larry enter and begin to play in another part of the stage. Douglas and Oliver move to a new position.)* Hugs, happy thoughts ... *(Hacks at weeds, looking for ball.)* Shit! *(Larry makes a great shot.)*

LARRY. Let the big dog eat!

OLIVER. *(Hands Douglas the ball.)* Here you are, old man.

DOUGLAS. Oh. *(Embarrassed; lightens up.)* Well, what can you do? Stop the woman from reading?

OLIVER. An excellent idea. A sick woman should never be exposed to medical information which can only confuse an already weakened and gullible mind. Have you applied leeches?

DOUGLAS. Thank you, Oliver. If I need a second opinion ... *(Ken makes a bad shot.)*

KEN. Fore!

OLIVER. Well, what *did* you do?

DOUGLAS. *(Utterly frustrated.)* Stage four breast cancer, Oliver! I'm a doctor — a surgeon — and I couldn't do a goddamn thing! What can you do? *(Beat; sighs.)* I told the nurse to give her a hug. *(Larry's cell phone rings. His "Hello" is cool and commanding. When he hears his wife's voice, he shrinks.)*

LARRY. *(Into phone.)* Hello — ... Well, I'm in a meeting right now, sweetie — *(Plaintively.)* I *did* do the "Listening" exercise! Well, *I* thought I was listening. Dr. Jeff thought I was listening ... *(At a loss.)* Well, I'm listening now, sweetie. Bye-bye. *(Douglas and Larry both make bad shots.)*

DOUGLAS.	LARRY.
Oh God.	Fore!

(Douglas and Larry see each other.)

LARRY. Doug!

DOUGLAS. Larry!

LARRY. How you hittin' 'em?

DOUGLAS. Terrific!

LARRY. Great! You remember Ken.

KEN. Dougie!

DOUGLAS. *(Doesn't remember him.)* No ... *(Introducing.)* Larry, Oliver —

OLIVER. Dr. Oliver Smoot. Pleased to meet you, Dr. —

LARRY. *(Laughs.)* Oh, I'm not a doctor. Just a businessman.

DOUGLAS. Larry's on the board of our hospital.

LARRY. And this is —

KEN. Ken Fine. I was in research at SMI, remember?

DOUGLAS. No …

KEN. *(To Oliver.)* I was at NCI after NIH — now I'm with the FDA.

OLIVER. *(Impressed but clueless.)* Jolly good!

DOUGLAS. *(With some urgency.)* Think we can get together this week, Larry? I was wondering if the board has decided about that new cancer treatment —

KEN. What new cancer treatment — ?

LARRY. *(Overlaps.)* Have your girl give my girl a call. *(He puts an arm around Ken, leading him off.)*

DOUGLAS. I'll call you! *(He makes his next shot. It's ridiculously easy, and, amazingly, he gets the ball in the hole.)* Beauty! So. Where do you want to eat?

OLIVER. *(Checks watch.)* I have to remove a colon in an hour … Steakhouse?

DOUGLAS. Fine. *(They go off. Sound of birds.)*

Scene 5

Douglas' office. On his desk is a picture of his wife with the family cat.

Wanda is seated, smoking. She puts out the cigarette and waves the smoke away, as Douglas enters, lost in her chart.

DOUGLAS. *(Cheery.)* Good afternoon.

WANDA. *(Rises, relieved.)* Oh good.

DOUGLAS. I beg your pardon?

WANDA. You said it was a good afternoon. So I guess that means I don't have the Big C.

DOUGLAS. Oh. I see. *(Pleasantly.)* Please, sit down, Ms. … *(Reads chart.)* Koznicki.

WANDA. Why? I mean, I don't want to be rude, but I just started a new job and —

DOUGLAS. *(Reading chart.)* You work at Haver Chemicals in New Jersey ... Do you handle pesticides?

WANDA. Nah, not anymore. Not for years. In fact, I have recently returned to Haver in an executive secretarial capacity — I have a very spacious cubicle — and I've already lost half a day's pay, so I'd love to chat, but —

DOUGLAS. Please sit down, Ms. Koznicki. You're not making this easy for me.

WANDA. Why? What's your problem? All you have to say is, "Wanda" — and please call me Wanda, any man who's worked me over like you have at least gets to call me Wanda — so all you have to say is, "Wanda, you're fine. No leaks, no lumps, please pay the nice nurse, and I never want to see you again as long as we both shall live, which in your case, Wanda, is gonna be a hell of a long time." Right?

DOUGLAS. I don't see why not —

WANDA. *(Laughs; sits.)* Whew. You kinda had me going there, doc.

DOUGLAS. *(Opening appointment book.)* Now the first thing I'd like to do is schedule a biopsy.

WANDA. Whoa. Wait a minute. You said it was a good afternoon.

DOUGLAS. Shall I continue?

WANDA. Can you sing "Feelings" instead? *(She laughs. Douglas looks perplexed.)* I'm sorry. I'm sorry, doc. I'm not making this easy for you. That mammogram ... I didn't take such a good picture, huh?

DOUGLAS. I'm afraid not.

WANDA. Why are *you* afraid?

DOUGLAS. Ms. Koznicki, we don't even know that the tumor is —

WANDA. I'm sorry, did somebody say "tumor"?

DOUGLAS. *(Thrown.)* Oh — well — *(An effort to cheer.)* As I was saying, we don't know that it is malignant until we do the biopsy. Now how is Tuesday, is Tuesday good?

WANDA. Tuesday. I was going to get a haircut on my lunch hour, but I guess a biopsy would be good too ... *(Beat.)* What's a biopsy?

DOUGLAS. We'll excise the tumor to see if it's malignant, or, hopefully, benign.

WANDA. Oh. *(Beat.)* What's "excise"?

DOUGLAS. Remove. With a scalpel. If everything looks all right, we'll have you back at work bright and early the next day.

WANDA. And if everything doesn't?

DOUGLAS. *(Checks book.)* Well, since you're concerned about time ... *(Glad to accommodate.)* If you like, we *could* schedule the biopsy so that, if necessary, surgery could be performed right then and there. *(He reaches for the phone.)*

WANDA. *(Jumps up.)* No, no, I don't think I'd like that. I don't think I'd like that at all. I think I'd just as soon opt for the haircut, and let me tell you, Mr. Juan can really butcher you if he's in a snit.

DOUGLAS. Mr. ... Juan?

WANDA. He's very good. He's the only man in New York who knows the meaning of "Just a *trim.*" Most guys just want to get in there and — *(She mimes cutting.)*

DOUGLAS. Ms. Koznicki —

WANDA. Also, I figure the haircut's more in my price range, seeing as how my insurance doesn't kick in for another *ten weeks and three days.*

DOUGLAS. I understand. *(Looks at watch.)* Now, why don't we just see how that biopsy works out, and then we can discuss further options.

WANDA. Good. Options sounds good. You know I went to this joint for lunch that had twenty-three kinds of burgers? You ever had a Belgian burger served between two Belgian waffles?

DOUGLAS. Uh ... I might cut down on the red meat.

WANDA. I might too! So. Options sounds good right?

DOUGLAS. *(With true conviction.)* Ms. Koznicki, we are testing promising new treatments all the time. This hospital happens to be one of the finest research centers in the world. I assure you, if options are to be found, you will find them here.

WANDA. *(À la the game shows.)* Wow! Is there a dishwasher behind that door? *(She takes out her cigarettes. Douglas waves a finger.)*

DOUGLAS. *(Rises.)* In any event, until I see the lab reports, all I can offer is an educated opinion based on the mammogram and my own examination.

WANDA. Yeah, well. *(Rises.)* I'm the kind of gal that waits till Oscar night, doc. I don't read the polls in *People* magazine. I don't care how many thumbs Siskel and Whatsisname get up, I wait till they open the envelope. I don't want an opinion, I want to know who the winner is!

DOUGLAS. That certainly is your decision. Any other questions I can answer for you right now?

WANDA. Yeah. Where's the nearest bar?

DOUGLAS. There's a bar right across from the hospital.

WANDA. *(After a beat.)* You know, someday, doc, we're gonna have a health care system in this country ... with a bar right *in* the hospital. *(She leaves.)*

Scene 6

A steam room. Douglas is lying down. Ken and Larry are seated. Larry is telling jokes, and he and Ken are laughing.

LARRY. Okay, got another. What's white — and ten inches? *(Waits; laughs.)* Nothing! *(Ken and Larry laugh.)* Okay, one more. Cancer patient comes in —

KEN. *(Laughs.)* You know, I think I know this —

LARRY. Doctor says, "I got good news and bad news, which do you want to hear first?"

KEN. *(Laughs.)* Oh, he wants the good —

LARRY. *(Cuts him off.)* Ken, you're ruining my joke.

DOUGLAS. *(Weary.)* Go ahead, Larry.

LARRY. All right. Patient says, "Give me the good news first."

KEN. See? I guessed right.

DOUGLAS. That's why you work for the FDA.

LARRY. Who do I have to fuck to tell a joke around here? *(Douglas points to Ken.)* Thank you. All right, doctor says, "The good news is you've got six months to live — "

DOUGLAS. Lucky man. What kind of cancer are we talking about here?

LARRY. Will you give me a break? I don't know, it's a joke! This isn't a real patient, Douglas, it's a joke patient!

DOUGLAS. Good.

LARRY. That's what he says! "Good, terrific, I got six months to live! Fantastic."

KEN. And the bad news?

LARRY. *(Dryly.)* Thank you for asking, Ken. Doctor says, "The bad news is I forgot to tell you six months ago." *(Larry and Ken laugh. Douglas sits up.)*

DOUGLAS. *(After a beat.)* So it's the doctor's fault.

LARRY. Douglas — it's a joke!

DOUGLAS. At the doctor's expense.

KEN. I thought it was pretty good.

DOUGLAS. Well, you're not doctors. You're a businessman, Larry, joke about money. *(To Ken.)* You're a scientist, joke about ... protozoa. *(Larry gets up, goes to the door, calls out to the Attendant.)*

LARRY. Honey, would you bring three glasses of water? Perrier? *(Attendant enters.)*

KEN. And a Tylenol? *(Beat.)* No ... make that an aspirin. *(Beat.)* Uh — better make it a Tylenol. If you have it. *(Attendant smiles and leaves.)*

DOUGLAS. How many FDA people does it take to screw in a light bulb?

KEN. How many?

DOUGLAS. Not "how many?" The question is, "how long?" *(Ken and Larry laugh.)*

LARRY. Good one, Dougie!

DOUGLAS. So what has the board decided about that new — cancer treatment? *(The Attendant, a black Puerto Rican woman, enters with glasses of water.)*

ATTENDANT. Here you are, *señor. (Lies.)* Perrier. And a Tylenol.

LARRY. Terrific. *(He lounges against the door seductively, blocking her way.)* Hola. Muy caliente. *(Toweling off.)* Ay, ay, caramba. *(They stare each other down a moment, and he "graciously" lets her pass.)*

ATTENDANT. *Gracias. (Smiles; leaving.)* Pendejo.

DOUGLAS. How's Catherine?

LARRY. Terrific! Judy?

DOUGLAS. She's fine. *(Beat; to Ken.)* And — ?

KEN. Lois. *(Beat.)* We're divorced.

DOUGLAS. Sorry. *(He turns to Larry and is about to speak.)*

KEN. Six months now. She got the house. The puppy — *(Douglas nods.)*

DOUGLAS. *(To Larry.)* So what has the board decided about that new cancer therapy —

KEN. So if you know anybody —

LARRY. Which one, Doug? There are so many these days.

KEN. I'm trying to get out more ...

DOUGLAS. The serum that Carson fellow's using in Jamaica. Are

31

we going to test it here at Smith Memorial? I've been hearing some encouraging reports.

KEN. *(Realizes.)* You know —

LARRY. From where, Dougie? I didn't know Carson's serum was legal in this country.

KEN. You know, I saw —

DOUGLAS. From my nurse. She worked at Carson's clinic in Jamaica for a while. Saw some excellent results.

LARRY. Oh. Good.

KEN. *Hello?* You know, when I was in research back in the eighties, I did a site visit for the National Cancer Institute. They were going to fund Carson's research here in New York —

DOUGLAS. They were?

KEN. Hold on a sec, Doug. And I saw his serum injected into mice with rock hard breast tumors, and I'm telling you, Lar, those tumors practically disappeared!

LARRY. Interesting ...

DOUGLAS. Was he funded?

KEN. Well, no —

DOUGLAS. Why the hell not?

KEN. Darndest thing. NCI offered the usual clinical trial — terminal patients, half would get the serum, half would get the placebo — *(Baffled.)* Carson refused — said it would be "inhumane" and "unethical" to give terminal patients a placebo.

DOUGLAS. And?

KEN. *(Shrugs.)* And the FDA turned down his request for an experimental permit.

DOUGLAS. Jesus. Why?

KEN. *(Paranoid.) I* don't know, I wasn't with the FDA at the time —

LARRY. *(The peacemaker.)* Fellas ...

KEN. We do have procedures, you know —

LARRY. Well, I love Jamaica ... *(Lightly.)* And you know, from what I've heard, Carson's serum isn't really all that different from INT-2, which Jones Pharmaceuticals is working on at Smith Memorial right now. And doing quite well with actually. *(Ken gets his inhaler.)*

DOUGLAS. But INT-2 is toxic, isn't it?

LARRY. All drugs have side effects —

DOUGLAS. Not Carson's serum apparently.

LARRY. *(Elbows Douglas.)* According to your nurse?

DOUGLAS. The girl's had two years of medical school, Larry.

LARRY. You boning her?

DOUGLAS. Am I — ? No. I just thought it would be interesting for us to give this a try, Larry. And I'd think you'd be interested too, as a member of the board of Smith Memorial ... if not as a vice president of Jones Pharmaceuticals — which stands to make a killing on INT-2.

KEN. *(Laughs.)* Doug —

LARRY. Well, I'm saddened that you see it that way.

KEN. *(Trying to keep the peace.)* Lar —

LARRY. Are you implying a conflict of interest, my friend?

KEN. Fellas —

LARRY. Because all sorts of companies are represented on the board of our hospital, Douglas, including the makers of petro-chemicals and tobacco, which, I believe, are known to *cause* cancer. Me, I'm in the business of a *cure*. Hell, I'm interested in anything that'll cure cancer. Apricot pits, vitamin C, ozone, "eye of newt and toe of frog."

DOUGLAS. This is not some quack cure. We're talking about a serum made from human blood. *(Larry's cellular phone rings.)*

LARRY. Excuse me. *(Into phone.)* Hello? Well, I'm in a meeting right now, sweetie ... Well, I did do the "Feelings" exercise ... Well, I thought I did the exercise ... Jeff thought I did the exercise ... *(Surprised, hurt.)* Those *were* my feelings! ... All right, I'll meet you in Jeff's office in an hour. *(He hangs up and goes back to Doug.)* Sorry, Doug, I'm listening. I'm hearing you.

DOUGLAS. Carson has isolated the proteins in the blood which the immune system uses to fight cancer. His theory is that — *(Ken jumps in to help.)*

KEN. In *lay* terms, Lar? You augment the immune system, and it'll cure its own cancer.

LARRY. Thank you, Ken.

KEN. No charge.

DOUGLAS. It's a non-toxic, non-invasive —

LARRY. Unproven — method.

DOUGLAS. Which is why I think we should do the tests.

LARRY. Well. *(Looks at watch; smiles.)* I certainly hear what you're saying about this, Doug. I hear you. And I'll be sure to speak to the board.

DOUGLAS. *(Surprised.)* You — ?

LARRY. So! Where do you want to eat?

DOUGLAS. *(Checks watch.)* Well, I have to operate on a toe in an hour ...

KEN. Chinese?

DOUGLAS. *(Hesitates.)* Fine.

Scene 7

Forgiveness' bedroom. Eighteenth-century China. A screen, a table, chair, and chaise.

Forgiveness is having dinner with her husband, Blessing From Heaven, whom she adores.

Haunting Chinese music in the background, Forgiveness' theme.

FORGIVENESS. Good trip? Much trade?

BLESSING. First Wife — *(Chuckles.)* They stab their dinner with fork and knife, their faces are covered with hair, they burn not only their women but their cats ... The English are barbarians. *(He puts down his chopsticks. Sexily.)* I am ready for dessert.

FORGIVENESS. *(Worried.)* Dessert?

BLESSING. I have been away a long time. *(He reaches for her foot, caresses it.)*

FORGIVENESS. *(Calls out quickly.)* Jade Ornament! *(The maid enters immediately, as if she'd been at the door, and bows.)* Dessert for the master.

JADE ORNAMENT. Two plates, master?

BLESSING. No plates. *(Jade Ornament raises an eyebrow and leaves. Blessing continues, lustily.)* Take off your shoes.

FORGIVENESS. All right ... *(Coy.)* Just one little shoe ... *(She takes off her left shoe.)*

BLESSING. Take off the other.

FORGIVENESS. You're not a young man, my husband. One at a time ... *(Blessing unwraps her left foot and caresses and smells it passionately. The maid enters with a bowl of lychees and stares, wide-eyed.)* You may go. Go! *(The maid runs for it, gagging. Forgiveness takes the lychee and places it on her toe. Blessing eats it off. The maid vomits offstage.)*

BLESSING. Delicious. My golden lotus … My golden lotus … I am ready for second helping. *(Reaches for Forgiveness' other foot.)* Take it off.

FORGIVENESS. No.

BLESSING. *(Husky.)* Yes.

FORGIVENESS. No, no …

BLESSING. Yes, yes. *(He grabs the right foot, pulls the shoe off, revealing a bloody bandage, and screams.)* What — what is this?

FORGIVENESS. Nothing, my husband. Little accident. Golden lotus … lost a petal — *(Blessing gets up. Forgiveness offers her good foot. Imploring.)* Doctor say I can still … Come, come finish your dessert, my Blessing. *(Blessing is angry and affronted, but mostly pained. He has love for Forgiveness, as well as for her foot.)*

BLESSING. Not … hungry. *(Forgiveness starts to serve tea.)*

FORGIVENESS. Tell me about your trip then. You stopped in Shanghai?

BLESSING. Yes.

FORGIVENESS. The weather was good?

BLESSING. Cold.

FORGIVENESS. And what did you bring home?

BLESSING. I brought silk for you, and candlesticks … spices … and another wife. *(The teapot trembles in Forgiveness' hand. She puts it down.)*

FORGIVENESS. *(Smiles.)* Yes? *(Beat.)* How old is she?

BLESSING. Eleven.

FORGIVENESS. She … is bound?

BLESSING. She comes from a poor family.

FORGIVENESS. But pretty?

BLESSING. I suppose …

FORGIVENESS. And what is the Fifth Wife's name, my husband?

BLESSING. Precious Snow. But I will call her Precious Swallow.

FORGIVENESS. Pretty. Like the springtime. *(She thinks. Blessing stands frozen, turned away from her.)* Bring her to me. So I can start the binding. Eleven is not too old.

BLESSING. *(Moved.)* Thank you.

FORGIVENESS. And did you bring back opium for your Forgiveness?

BLESSING. Of course. *(He claps for the maid. Jade Ornament brings the pipe and exits. He lights it for Forgiveness. She takes a long drag.)*
FORGIVENESS. Tomorrow we start the binding. *(Blessing touches her shoulder with tenderness and gratitude ... and leaves.)* Tomorrow lucky day by the moon ... *(She takes another drag. Leans back. Smiles.)*

Scene 8

An Eastside bar across from the hospital, à la Friday's. Music on the jukebox. Johnny is behind the bar. An angry Woman Lawyer (played by the actress who plays Victoria) is knocking back vodka, and reading the Times. *The Waitress (played by the actor who plays Larry) enters and goes to the bar. Ken enters, in business clothes, grooving to the music.*

KEN. Uh, Johnny, can I have a Long Island Ice Tea?
JOHNNY. And that's with Sweet'N Low, right, Ken?
KEN. Uh no — you might as well use sugar. Well — make it half sugar, half Sweet'N Low. *(Beat; worries.)* Johnny wait! No Sweet 'N Low.
JOHNNY. You got it. *(Ken cozies up to the Woman Lawyer.)*
KEN. So. You all ready for the weekend?
WOMAN LAWYER. *(Turns, fires.)* How DARE you? Of all the patriarchal, phallocentric, gynophobic — no, I am not ready for "the weekend." What is "the weekend"? Some puerile pornographic fantasy in which every woman in the world gets to be an extra? I am *not* ready for "the weekend"! I WILL NEVER BE READY FOR THE WEEKEND! *(She goes back to her paper.)*
KEN. Okay. Just wondered ... *(Wanda enters, sits at the bar, and lights a cigarette. Ken gets next to her. She blows smoke in his face.)*
WANDA. If this bothers you, feel free to move.
KEN. Oh, no problem. I mean, live and let live. *(He drops his keys to get a better angle on Wanda's breasts. To her breasts.)* So, you all ready for the weekend?
WANDA. They sure are.
KEN. Got plans?

WANDA. Sure do. First I'm gonna get drunk. *(To Johnny.)* Jack Daniel's. *(To Ken; enticing.)* And then I'm gonna do something I've wanted to do for a long time.

KEN. Hey, go for it. *(Wanda gets out of her seat and does a little shimmy to the music. Ken shimmies with her. She shimmies two steps closer — and bunts him with her rock-hard breasts. He reels.)* You know, you could've just said, "I'm waiting for somebody." *(He goes off to another part of the bar.)*

WANDA. I'm not a nice person. I'm gonna rot in hell. I better have another.

JOHNNY. *(Pouring.)* I better get another bottle. *(An Asian Cabbie runs in.)*

CABBIE. Hey, Johnny — got somebody in cab — you know where Folk Art Museum is?

JOHNNY. Nope.

CABBIE. Fuck 'em, gimme a bud. *(A Male Lawyer, played by the actor who plays Oliver, enters. He stands next to the Woman Lawyer. They are instantly attracted and repelled by each other.)*

MALE LAWYER. I'll have a dry Absolut martini on the rocks, with an olive.

WOMAN LAWYER. *(Glares and tops the Male Lawyer.)* I'll have an EXTRA DRY martini, STOLICHNAYA, straight up — WITH A TWIST!

JOHNNY. You got it. *(Brenda enters.)* Hi, Brenda.

BRENDA. Wha happen Johnny?

WANDA. Hi Brenda!

BRENDA. *(Dryly.)* Oh, hi. How you doin'?

WANDA. *(Smiles.)* Really wanna know?

BRENDA. *("Not really.")* Well, uh …

WANDA. Well, I'll tell you. I got home last night, I had six calls on my machine. Four of 'em from guys. *(A quick nod from Brenda.)*

WOMAN LAWYER. Duh … *(The Waitress brings Brenda a beer. Brenda takes out some books to study.)*

WANDA. See, I joined this video dating thing. *(Matter of fact.)* One's an extremely handsome, sensitive CEO who makes time for his many friends. One's in construction, but he likes long walks in the rain … One's Christian, and he only dates women between five eight and six one, which I don't think is very Christian of him, and they gotta be blonde but he'll consider a dyed blonde who accepts Jesus … *(Thrilled.)* And the last guy's a smoker.

BRENDA. *(Wry.)* Great —

WANDA. Plus, he doesn't want kids, he lives in Manhattan, he likes to eat in restaurants which is where I like to eat, and he doesn't jog. So I figure as long as he doesn't have bad breath, a record, or a fish on his car, this is it. The bet's up in thirty days. This is the guy.

BRENDA. *(What can she say?)* Great. *(She opens her books.)*

WOMAN LAWYER. Get a dog.

WANDA. See, I made a bet with my mother five years ago after I read this article she sent me from *Newsweek* while I was waiting to get a pap smear — *(Brenda tries to do her homework. Wanda includes the Woman Lawyer and Johnny.)* See, the article said the odds of my getting married by forty were not quite as good as the odds of my being shot by a terrorist. I wonder how come these articles never mention the possibility of the terrorist falling madly in love and wanting to marry you?

WOMAN LAWYER. *(Rises.)* Because they're written by *men*. The writers are *men*, the publishers are *men*, and the terrorists are MEN! *(She grabs her briefcase and leaves. The Waitress goes to the bar. Wanda includes her.)*

WANDA. So anyway, I bet my mother a hundred bucks I'd beat the odds, and I went to work.

WAITRESS. Well, you look fabulous —

WANDA. Yeah? I saw this modeling expert who said to divide my body in parts and go over it with a magnifying glass. Parts I could improve, I'd work on, and the rest I'd just cover up. So I started from the top. Hair, eyebrows —

WAITRESS. Well, you look *fabulous.*

MALE LAWYER. *(Flirts; sotto.)* As do you —

WANDA. *(To Waitress.)* Yeah? You should have seen the Visa bills. Luckily, I had a couple of boyfriends along the way who were very — supportive, if not marriage material. One even started to pay for my second pair of tits, but he was a recovering cocaine addict and he had a slip … and he got fired from the police department. But he was really spiritual, and he told me this prayer about "accepting stuff I cannot change"? And to just turn my breasts over to God, and God'd come up with the money for new tits.

JOHNNY. "God grant me the serenity — "

ALL BUT WANDA. " — to accept the things I cannot change, the courage to change the things I can, and the wisdom to know the difference."

WANDA. Right. *(Downs her drink.)* I'll have another. *(Working the room.)* So *then* I went to work on my weight! I did Weight Watchers, Nutrisystem, Jenny Craig ... Weight Watchers, Optifast, Overeaters Anonymous ... Weight Watchers, cocaine, and finally lipo. Then I met this writer in a bar who wrote an article on me and the bet for *Self* magazine, and the most beautiful thing started happening. Women all over the country started sending me donations ... *(The bar starts humming a tune such as "We've Only Just Begun,"* as if accompanying Wanda.)* I got on *Oprah* — the Paramus Kawanis Club wants to give me their hall for my wedding! — The Vanity Fair Outlet is giving me a trousseau, Video Nuts is giving me and my husband a lifetime membership, the Taj Mahal in Atlantic City is donating the bridal suite! — I even got a letter from my local councilman — I was like, hey, even the government wants me to win! So now I got thirty days to find the guy — and this morning I go to the doctor ... *(Beat.)* And I got a tumor. *(Downs drink; to Brenda.)* And that's how I'm doin'. *(Ken coughs once and exits. The Cabbie coughs twice and exits. The Male Lawyer coughs three times and exits. The Waitress and Ken exit too. Cancer has cleared the bar. To Johnny.)* I'll have another. *(Brenda sighs and gets up.)*
BRENDA. I'll buy you another. Let's go. *(Brenda takes Wanda's arm and leads her out. A light change, traffic sounds, and they're in the park.)*

Scene 9

Central Park. Brenda hands Wanda a cup.

BRENDA. Here. Have a drink.
WANDA. *(Disappointed.)* Coffee?
BRENDA. *("Cover your mouth.")* Kibba yu mout and drink it. I'm a nurse, it's good for you.
WANDA. Like taking a walk in Central Park?
BRENDA. I like the park. Reminds me of nature. *(Rap music passes. Something harsh.)*

---

* See Special Note on Songs and Recordings on copyright page.

WANDA. What the hell. Maybe I'll get mugged and miss my biopsy.
BRENDA. Don't worry. We can fill your appointment. *(Points into audience.)* See that building there? Four out of five apartments got someone inside with cancer, or waiting to get it —
WANDA. Jees, I thought you were a happy island kinda people.
BRENDA. Chu man, I say this to cheer you up. We don't even know you got cancer. Where you goin' get cancer? You don't have a single body part that's real.
WANDA. *(Laughs.)* Right! You know, I hate the park. Where's the subway? *(Wanda turns and sees Victoria, who has just entered U., reading Freud. She wears a coat over her nightgown, as if she'd run out of the house, and she's smoking a cigar.)*
VICTORIA. Hmmm … And the obsessive thought "I desire to murder you," on further analysis, means "I should like to make love to you."
WANDA. Hey! How ya doin'? *(Victoria turns and sees them.)*
VICTORIA. *(Caught.)* Oh — hello! Lovely evening. The park, the night air … *(She takes a deep breath, and coughs horribly.)* It gets so humid in the house, what with the children and all …
BRENDA. Mrs. Smoot, what are you — ?
VICTORIA. Oh. Well. My husband was called away on an emergency, and I thought I'd — take a walk. *(Bit defiant.)* With Freud.
BRENDA. That a cigar?
VICTORIA. *(Hides it.)* This? Oh no, no. *(She sits on the bench. Graciously.)* Won't you sit down?
WANDA. I really gotta —
BRENDA. Sit. *(Brenda leads Wanda to the bench and they sit.)* How's the hysteria, Mrs. Smoot?
VICTORIA. Progressing, actually. I bit the maid. *(Beat.)* And the gardener. And a young boy in our church choir. Well, he was dreadfully off-key.
BRENDA. *(Laughs; approving.)* Eh eh.
VICTORIA. And the pastor. And the butcher gave me chicken livers instead of beef. And, of course, my *(Flings arm.)* — husband. My husband wonders if a hysterectomy might not be prescribed now too. The uterus. Along with the ovaries. Since I'll be in the hospital for the ovaries —

BRENDA.	VICTORIA.
Well, as long as you're —	As long as I'm there.

(Rap music passes. Victoria jumps up.)

40

VICTORIA. SHUT UP! Stop that insufferable noise this instant! *(Regroups.)* Well, there's no melody!

WANDA. Boy, you two really are a hoot, aren't you? You are just the kind of gals I like to party with. Especially after a nice visit to the doctor. Thank you so much for dragging me out of that awful bar. *(Rises.)* This has really been fun. *(She starts to walk away.)*

BRENDA. We see you Tuesday then?

WANDA. Tuesday?

BRENDA. Biopsy? *(Forgiveness appears and begins a long slow hobble around the periphery of the stage, unseen by the others. She carries a suitcase along with her cane. Wanda turns to Brenda.)*

WANDA. Look, what do you know, anyway? You're not a doctor, you're just a nurse.

BRENDA. *(Smiles.)* My mother was a doctor! Cured hernias, migraine, hemorrhoids ... broken hearts. She could make a man love you by lighting a cigar, blowin' smoke down your body, writin' his name, and stickin' it with your pubic hair in an empty tuna can. You ought to try it, chile.

VICTORIA. I'm sorry. Your mother was...?

WANDA. Mom was a witch. Great.

BRENDA. I'm just a witch-nurse now. But I'll be a witch-doctor some day. Went to two years of medical school in Jamaica.

WANDA. In Jamaica?

VICTORIA. It's a colony. Of the crown.

BRENDA. I studied at George the Fifth Memorial Hospital.

WANDA. *("Tell me another.")* In Jamaica?

BRENDA. Near Half Way Tree.

WANDA. That where you come from? Half Way Tree?

BRENDA. No, chile. I come from Me No Send, You No Come.

WANDA. Uh-huh. So why didn't you finish med school?

BRENDA. Well, my mother ...

WANDA. *(Laughs.)* Put a hex on the teacher?

BRENDA. *(With difficulty.)* My mother ... got cancer. And she couldn't scare it away. Hmmmn-hmmmn. Doctors took a breast, it jumped to the other one. They took that, it jumped to the bones. Like a lizard with little feet. Quick little fucker. Doctors chasing it all over her body ...

VICTORIA. *(Reflexively polite.)* How is she?

BRENDA. Very well, thank you. *(Smiles; wry.)* Back at work cleaning houses.

VICTORIA. Oh good. *(She goes back to Freud.)*

BRENDA. And I'm taking night courses now. In Jersey. *(Wanda reluctantly smiles.)* You know, Ms. Kozinski, witches were healing with herbs when doctors were still getting their prognoses from the stars. 'Course they burned nine million witches — and their cats for good measure.

WANDA. Get real.

BRENDA. There were no cats left to eat the rats, plague came along, and the world went to hell in a — *(Searches.)* pocketbook.

VICTORIA. "Handbasket."

BRENDA. Whatever. It got there. *(Laughs.)* Den give me a cigar, nuh! *(She holds out her hand to Victoria, who hands her a cigar and lights one for herself. To Wanda.)* And maybe this witch-nurse will tell you 'bout a doctor down Jamaica way. Cures with a blood potion. A witch-doctor, some say. *(Puffing.)* What do you say, Ms. Kozynski? After what you done to your body, a little talk ain't goin' kill you. *(After a moment, Wanda holds out her hand. Victoria gives her a cigar, and the three women smoke. Forgiveness enters the scene.)*

FORGIVENESS. *(Brightly.)* Hello!

VICTORIA. How are you?

FORGIVENESS. Oh, fine. Just taking little walk in the forest.

VICTORIA. *(Regards her foot.)* Painful, I'd imagine.

FORGIVENESS. *(Laughs.)* Oh, terrible!

BRENDA. How come you're carrying that suitcase, Mrs. From Heaven?

FORGIVENESS. *(Lies.)* Oh … Husband … sleeping. Didn't want to wake him! Pretty night, huh? Many stars. *(She sits on her suitcase, takes out her pipe.)* Somebody got a light? *(Wanda kneels next to her and lights her pipe.)*

WANDA. Wait a minute. You see stars? In the park?

FORGIVENESS. Got to be there. Where else they gonna be? *(Points.)* You see the moon? Just 'cause you see piece of it, don't mean rest is not there. Luck is like that, huh? Just hiding sometimes … Once bandits came and made all the bound women in my house dance on a field of rocks till rocks were covered with blood. Some women were tied up so legs dangled in air, and bricks were tied around each toe till they straightened and dropped off.

VICTORIA. You were …

42

FORGIVENESS. In town. Shopping.

WANDA. Shopping?

FORGIVENESS. Lucky, huh? *(The women nod.)*

WANDA. *(With wonder.)* Yeah ...

FORGIVENESS. Oh, sometimes luck hiding for looong time ... *(She looks up. One by one, four stars appear in the sky. The women sit, looking out, smoking.)*

End of Act One

ACT TWO

Scene 1

Two massage tables. Dreamy new age music. An Asian Masseuse works on Ken. An African-American Masseuse works on Larry, who is telling a joke.

LARRY. So this guy's waiting on line to get into heaven ... And a guy in a white coat goes to the front of the line — and gets right in. So the first guy says to the guard, "How come that doctor just walks right in like that?" And the guard says, "Oh, that's no doctor. That's God. *(Beat.)* He just *thinks* he's a doctor!" *(They both laugh. The masseuses don't.)*

KEN. Oh, that's good, Larry. *(To masseuse.)* Can you go a little harder, hon? *(Asian Masseuse goes harder.)* Ow — not quite that hard.

LARRY. *(A compliment.)* You working out, Ken?

KEN. Uh — yeah. *(To masseuse.)* You're not using coconut oil are you?

ASIAN MASSEUSE. No coconut.

KEN. Okay.

LARRY. *(Beat; thoughtful.)* You know, Ken, it's not that I don't want to give Carson's serum a try. I just can't see wasting hard-won funding when we have a group at Smith Memorial right now working on something every bit as promising.

KEN. What — ?

LARRY. INT-2, Ken.

KEN. But how do you know it's as promising? If you're still working on it.

LARRY. Well, because, the fellow who developed it for us was on Carson's team in Jamaica for a while.

KEN. And now he works for you at Smith Memorial? *(This is just business as usual.)*

LARRY. Well, he works for Jones Pharmaceuticals. Smith Memorial is testing the drug for us.

KEN. *(Nods.)* So you'll share in the patent —

LARRY. But if the FDA were to approve Carson's serum —

KEN. You could lose the patent.

LARRY. *(With a little laugh.)* Well, *we* could lose the patent, Ken. You are a stockholder in Jones Pharmaceuticals —

KEN. *(Merely factual.)* Well, most of my stock's in tobacco —

LARRY. And, by the way, I'm speaking to you as a fellow stockholder — and, of course, as my friend. Listen, I know what you're going through. You should see *my* alimony payments!

AFRICAN-AMERICAN MASSEUSE. Relax, please.

KEN. Thanks. *(Beat.)* Have you told Doug about — ? *(As the Asian Masseuse works on Ken's feet, he is progressively turned on.)*

LARRY. *(Laughs.)* What does Doug have to do with this? He's a doctor. All he cares about is his patients. I'm on the board, I have a hospital to worry about. And people like Carson are eating up patients who could benefit from our services. So ... what do we do, Ken? *(Ken is elsewhere.)* Ken?

KEN. *(Startled.)* What?

LARRY. Well, I'll tell you one thought I did have. We make it known that Carson's serum may be contaminating patients with AIDS and hepatitis.

KEN. You're joking. It is?

LARRY. I said, "it may be." After all, we're talking about a serum made from human blood.

KEN. How did you find this out?

LARRY. I'll tell you how we *could* find this out. You — the FDA, that is — requests samples of Carson's serum.

KEN. Why?

LARRY. Because it may be contaminated.

KEN. But — what if it isn't contaminated?

LARRY. Well, I'm not a scientist, so correct me if I'm wrong — but it's my understanding that if we don't find AIDS antibodies via the usual tests, it could be cultured from Carson's serum. *(The women's work begins to reflect their feelings about the conversation.)*

KEN. What? You can't do that, Larry. I'm sorry.

LARRY. Well, like I said, I'm not a scientist. *(Laughs.)* I didn't even get into med school —

KEN. *(The scientist.)* Okay. First of all, it's just not that unusual to find AIDS antibodies in blood or blood products. Take gamma globulin —

LARRY. Really?

KEN. *(Nods.)* Made from blood collected from *thousands* of donors — if one donor has AIDS antibodies, the whole darn pool tests positive!

LARRY. Gee, does the public know that?

KEN. *(Defensive.)* Of course not! Why? Are you suggesting the FDA tell them? What for? In making gamma globulin the AIDS virus is killed.

LARRY. But in making Carson's serum?

KEN. Who knows? I don't know a darn thing about making his serum!

ASIAN MASSEUSE. Relax, please. *(The masseuse makes Larry's massage rather uncomfortable as he continues.)*

LARRY. How *could* you know? And that's all you have to say. "We don't know." It's an unproven method — *(His phone rings. He doesn't pause.)* I'll let that ring. And you direct customs and postal authorities to detain any serum being brought into the country. Just as you did with laetrile and all the other quack cures. *(To masseuse.)* Watch the nails, sweetheart. Ken — someone could get sick!

KEN. Someone could …

LARRY. A cancer patient! You know how vulnerable these people are — they're like children! Just promise them some magic herb that will make all the pain go away … No side effects at all, and they can keep their hair. It's just unconscionable — it just breaks my heart how these people are played on.

KEN. Tell me about it —

LARRY. And you are in a position — you have the *power* to protect these folks —

KEN. *(Distressed.)* Heck, they don't know what to take — and the doctors don't know what the heck to give 'em —

LARRY. That's up to you —

KEN. Well, I'm the government, aren't I? What are we supposed to do? Let any darn thing into the country?

LARRY. I think not.

KEN. *(To Masseuse.)* You know, I think I smell coconut —

BOTH MASSEUSES. No coconut!

KEN. Are you sure? *(They nod. With authority.)* All right. *(He lies back down. The women make quick staccato slaps up and down the men's backs, building like a drumbeat. Ken thinks. Inspired now.)* You know, if that new drug of yours is only *half* as effective as what Carson was using a decade ago ... That patent —

LARRY. *(Stops him.)* Ken — it's not the money. The bottom line is not the money. *(With true passion.)* I'm going to *cure* cancer ... *(Slow fade.)*

Scene 2

The Waiting Room. Canned music, as usual.

Wanda is alone, reading Glamour *intently. Victoria enters, greatly agitated.*

VICTORIA. My dear —

WANDA. Hey. Hold on, I'm reading an article about breasts. *(Victoria tries to compose herself. She sits, gets up, paces. Finally she can't stand it anymore.)*

VICTORIA. I'm terribly sorry to disturb you, I, ah ... wanted to return that book to you, the ah *(Sneezes.)* — Freud.

WANDA. Okay.

VICTORIA. But I'm afraid that ... My husband and I were discussing Freud's theories, you see, and my husband, quite accidentally, of course ... dropped Freud. Into the fire.

WANDA. Well, don't worry about it. There's a Barnes and Noble downstairs. You want another copy?

VICTORIA. Oh no! Thank you, I couldn't possibly. Unless ... perhaps I could give you some money — and I could perhaps just — read a few books here, while I'm waiting.

WANDA. Ya want me to do a book deal for you? Run books? *(Victoria takes a long list from her bosom and hands it to Wanda.)*

VICTORIA. I'd be ever so grateful. *(Hands over her purse.)* Do get yourself a few as well. And hurry! Please. I'd like to finish Freud by my appointment.

WANDA. Why?

VICTORIA. Well, you see I, ah ... I bit — I bit — I bit my husband's ...

WANDA. No! You bit his —

VICTORIA. *(Distraught.)* I bit his nose! And now he's wondering if a few teeth might not be removed as well. Along with the uterus. And the ovaries, of course. Perhaps he was just in a foul mood, but if I can just figure out what's wrong with me, I'm quite sure I can convince the doctor my problems are in my *mind!*

WANDA. Oh, I get it. Kinda like copping a plea.

VICTORIA. I beg your pardon?

WANDA. *(Rises.)* I'll get Freud. What the hell, I'm in no rush. *(Victoria takes a romance novel from under her skirt. Wanda starts to leave as Forgiveness enters, carrying a suitcase — a large round Chinese basket about three feet high.)*

FORGIVENESS. Hello.

WANDA. Hey!

FORGIVENESS. Pretty dress.

WANDA. Oh, thank you. Great *(Searches.)* ... purse. *(She leaves. Forgiveness sits.)*

VICTORIA. How are you?

FORGIVENESS. Oh, fine. *(Picks leaves from her hair.)* Pretty outfit!

VICTORIA. Yes, well, the doctor says the corset's compressing my stomach, dislocating the kidneys, crushing my liver, and constricting the heart — but it is pretty, isn't it? Your husband?

FORGIVENESS. With ... other wives.

VICTORIA. Nice for you. Your children?

FORGIVENESS. Exhausting.

VICTORIA. *(Sniffs.)* Your foot?

FORGIVENESS. Little problem with big toe.

VICTORIA. Well, I'm sure the doctor will fix it.

FORGIVENESS. Fell off this morning.

VICTORIA. Heavens to Betsy!

FORGIVENESS. Doctor might have to amputate.

VICTORIA. Oh dear.

FORGIVENESS. *(Smiles.)* What I need a foot for, at my age? *(Douglas rushes in — then looks around, lost.)*

DOUGLAS. Oh —

FORGIVENESS. Hello.

DOUGLAS. I'm sorry. I must have — used the wrong door. I —

VICTORIA. Won't you sit down?

DOUGLAS. *(Rather aghast.)* Sit down? Thank you ... No. *(He leaves.)*

48

Scene 3

Larry's office. Larry is on the headphone, bound by a long wire, to his wife. A statue of the Venus de Milo graces his desk.

LARRY. *(Trying; nicely.)* Uh-hunh ... Uh-huh ... Well, I hear what you're saying, sweetie, and I can certainly empathize with — ... Well, I don't think it's necessary to reiterate what you ... Ca — I think what Jeff meant when he said we should "mirror each other's feelings" was that we — ... No, not that we reiterate — hold on a sec, sweetie — *(Loudly, to an imaginary interruption.)* Yes? Did you want something, Phyllis? I'm talking to my wife. *(He mumbles a quick, high pitched "Phyllis" response. The last word, and only distinguishable word, is "meeting." Into phone.)* Sorry, sweetie — *(To "Phyllis.")* Well, then the board will just have to wait, Phyllis. Just tell the board that I am speaking with my wife and they will have to wait. *(He mumbles "Phyllis's" retort. The last words are "get angry." Into phone.)* So who's this new doctor you want to go see? ... Deepak Chopper? ... *("Interested.")* What's his theory? *(Takes a pill as she explains.)* Three kinds of body types, kapha, vatta, pitta ... You're a kapha, I'm a what? ... A pitta? ... I'm not a pitta, Cathy ... I'm not a pitta. *(Plaintive.)* Because it sounds like "pitiful"! *(Cerise, an attractive French secretary, enters. Larry covers mouthpiece.)* What is it, Cerise?
CERISE. *(Slow and sexy.)* Dr. McCaskill is here.
LARRY. Great. Send him in. And bring us a couple of Pellegrinos.
CERISE. *Très bien. (She lingers, flirting.)*
LARRY. Love that blouse, Cerise, *très* chic. *(Cerise laughs throatily, and very slowly and sexily leaves. He uncovers the mouthpiece.)* Well, I'm not going to see him. Because I'm sick of being the pitta in this relationship, Cathy! I don't want to see Dr. Chopper, or Dr. Jeff — I'm sick of doctors! I don't want to see them or listen to their tapes in my car — and if I want to listen to some philosopher with an accent, I'll take a CAB! ... Fine! Call your lawyer! *(Douglas enters. Sweetly.)* And kiss the twins for me. I love you too. *(Hangs up.)* Doug! I wasn't expecting to see you till — our game's Friday, isn't it?

DOUGLAS. It is.

LARRY. Well, sit down. Sit. Good to see you. How are you?

DOUGLAS. Not bad. How's the family?

LARRY. Terrific. Judy?

DOUGLAS. Fine.

LARRY. Say, have you heard the one about the doctor's wife who goes in for a —

DOUGLAS. Yes, I have. It's funny.

LARRY. Yeah, I thought so too. So what brings you all the way upstairs? *(Cerise slinks in with drinks and gives Douglas the once-over.)* Thank you, Cerise. Now if you don't mind, my lover and I would like to be alone. *(Cerise laughs long and knowingly, and leaves.)* So.

DOUGLAS. I'm still waiting to hear whether we're going to do those tests on Carson's serum, Larry.

LARRY. Doug — you haven't heard? Carson's clinic's been closed down.

DOUGLAS. What?!

LARRY. Just temporarily, I'm sure. Something about tainted serum — AIDS scare. The FDA got a hold of some samples —

DOUGLAS. How many samples were contaminated?

LARRY. *Possibly* contaminated. I think they're making an awfully big deal about it myself.

DOUGLAS. How many samples were possibly contaminated?

LARRY. Looks like … one — so far. But the Jamaican government just freaked. Well, they live off tourism down there, so you really can't blame them. And you know how people get when they hear the word AIDS.

DOUGLAS. But a clinic is never closed down in this manner. Usually they're informed of the problem, they correct it and go on. It doesn't make sense. Does it make sense to you?

LARRY. No, but I didn't close the clinic. The Jamaicans did. What is it with you and this serum anyway? I've never known you to be so —

DOUGLAS. I'm just tired of seeing new treatments cut off at the … God, I'm trying to think of something I haven't cut off this week.

LARRY. I understand how you feel.

DOUGLAS. Do you?

LARRY. Well — I can certainly empathize with —

DOUGLAS. With what?

LARRY. Well, I don't think it's necessary to reiterate —

DOUGLAS. But I haven't said —

LARRY. Dou — *(They keep cutting each other off.)*

DOUGLAS. So what are you —

LARRY. Dou —

DOUGLAS. La —

LARRY. Dou —

DOUGLAS. La —

LARRY. *(Laughs.)* Douglas! What I'm *trying* to understand is why this is so important to you all of a sudden? You sure it doesn't have to do with that nurse of yours?

DOUGLAS. No.

LARRY. Dougie, we went to school together —

DOUGLAS. Twenty years ago.

LARRY. Well, I'm saddened that you see it that way.

DOUGLAS. It has nothing to do with my nurse.

LARRY. Oh ... I get it. *(Smiles.)* You weren't investing in Carson's clinic — ?

DOUGLAS. No.

LARRY. Because I could certainly understand if maybe —

DOUGLAS. *(Overlaps.)* Maybe I have cancer. *(There is a pause.)*

LARRY. Don't kid about this, Doug. Not about this. It's not funny.

DOUGLAS. It's not conclusive.

LARRY. *(Truly concerned.)* What does your doctor say?

DOUGLAS. I haven't seen one.

LARRY. What ... what kind?

DOUGLAS. Prostate.

LARRY. Prostate? Christ. My father ... *(He swallows and goes to the phone.)* Well — thank God we have the best surgeons in town —

DOUGLAS. Fuck surgery! Not within a mile of *my* goddamn dick! Would you do surgery, Larry?

LARRY. Well, I ... I'd have to speak with my doctor —

DOUGLAS. Carson claims that nine of his cases have improved and gone home without surgery.

LARRY. *(Shaken.)* Doug — our — our people are working on new treatments all the time. INT-2 looks very — promising. We're working —

DOUGLAS. When, Larry?

LARRY. Day and night. We're going to beat this, Dougie.

DOUGLAS. When are we going to beat this?

LARRY. Soon. I promise you. We will beat this! *(He goes to hug Douglas.)*

DOUGLAS. That's okay, Larry. Last thing I need right now is a hug. *(He hands Larry the Pellegrino and leaves.)*

Scene 4

The doctor's office. Douglas rushes in, followed by Brenda. He changes out of his coat and into his doctor's jacket, and picks up the phone.

DOUGLAS. Give me a minute, and send in the next patient.

BRENDA. All right. *(Concerned.)* Do you need anything?

DOUGLAS. I'm fine. *(Brenda nods and leaves. Into phone.)* Dr. Fisher please, Dr. McCaskill calling, and no I cannot hold ... Thank you ... *(Tries to sound cheery.)* Ben? Doug. I was wondering if I could drop by and see you ... This afternoon, if you have time ... Five o'clock is fine. Thanks. *(He hangs up and dials again. When he hears his wife's voice, he is filled with love and concern for her.)* Judy? *(Trying not to break.)* How are you, sweetheart? ... No no, I'm fine. I'm going to be a little late for dinner is all, I have an appointment in the city ... Uh-huh, I see ... Well, what did the new vet say? ... *(Sinks into chair.)* The cat has stress? ... No, sweetheart, if she's still not using the litter box, I — I guess the acupuncture is certainly worth a try. *(Wanda enters. Into phone.)* I'll talk to the old vet, and we can compare — *(Sees Wanda.)* We'll discuss it when I get home ... Love you too. Bye-bye. *(Hangs up.)* Good afternoon, Ms. Koznicki.

WANDA. *(Laughs; sits.)* Oh, no you don't. You tell me. *(Douglas pauses, composing himself. This time he looks at her.)*

DOUGLAS. I'm afraid that the tumor did prove malignant. I'd like to schedule you for surgery as soon as possible. *(It takes a moment for Wanda to take that in.)*

WANDA. Surgery? You mean lumpe — lumpectomy? I've been reading —

DOUGLAS. I'm afraid that, due to the size of the tumor, lumpectomy is not a feasible option. Perhaps if it had been found earlier —

WANDA. Look, I had a mammogram last year.

DOUGLAS. Sometimes, in the case of women who have implants —

WANDA. They ... hog the picture. Yeah, I read that in *Glamour.*

DOUGLAS. As you can see from your recent mammogram, we're developing better procedures for mammography all the time —

WANDA. Oh good. That's good.

DOUGLAS. In the meantime ... I'm afraid the breast will have to be removed. *(There is a pause.)*

WANDA. *(Pointed.)* "The" breast? You mean — *my* breast?

DOUGLAS. Uh — yes. Fortunately, with reconstructive surgery, you can look quite normal.

WANDA. What — *(Beat; incredulous.)* implants?!

DOUGLAS. I assure you they are perfectly legal in cases such as your own.

WANDA. Whoa. You're gonna take out my implants, and my — breast — and give me — IMPLANTS?

DOUGLAS. *Saline* implants, of course. Made from salt water.

WANDA. Where do they get the water? Jersey Shore?

DOUGLAS. The solution is quite sterile, I assure you.

WANDA. Well, how do they get the water in there? Shots? What is it — like a water bed?

DOUGLAS. They're in a casing.

WANDA. Of what?

DOUGLAS. Well ... silicone. Ms. Koznicki, silicone is in everything these days, even baby food.

WANDA. Oh, I don't think so. Not this time.

DOUGLAS. Of course, it's your decision. No one is forcing you to —

WANDA. And no one can force me to have the masec — the maste —

DOUGLAS. Mastectomy.

WANDA. No one can force me to have that either.

DOUGLAS. We're not talking about an elective procedure. This procedure can save your life!

WANDA. What about this doctor I've been hearing about in Jamaica? *(Douglas is stunned.)*

DOUGLAS. Where did you hear about this?

WANDA. Hey, I read.

DOUGLAS. This doctor hasn't published.

WANDA. All right, I heard about it in Central Park.

DOUGLAS. I'm afraid this treatment is what the FDA calls an "unproven method."

WANDA. I bet mold didn't look too proven until it was proven to be penicillin —

DOUGLAS. I'm afraid you are not a good candidate for this treatment. Even if it were proven, even if it were legal in this country, which it is not.

WANDA. I've always wanted to see Jamaica —

DOUGLAS. First of all, they're ... not taking new patients right now. And second of all, you don't have time. You need this operation. As soon as possible.

WANDA. You mean as soon as my insurance kicks in. See, I got a little money from my mother's life insurance — but I was saving that for a rainy day —

DOUGLAS. Ms. Koznicki —

WANDA. KOZYNSKI!

DOUGLAS. You have what appears to be a very aggressive tumor.

WANDA. Do I? *(Hard.)* Sorry.

DOUGLAS. Any other questions I can answer for you right now? *(There is a pause. Wanda takes a pack of cigarettes from her purse.)*

WANDA. *(Challenging, wry.)* Yeah. Why me?

DOUGLAS. *(Refers to Wanda's chart.)* Well, uh, you have a number of known risk factors. Heredity, alcohol consumption, your job —

WANDA. What's riskier — working or getting born?

DOUGLAS. I was referring to your previous chemical exposure — shall I go on?

WANDA. Yeah.

DOUGLAS. Early menstruation, diet, smoking — *(Wanda puts the cigarettes down on his desk.)* Lack of childbearing —

WANDA. Woops —

DOUGLAS. On the other hand, in eighty percent of breast cancer cases, the women have no known risk factors at all, so —

WANDA. All you know is it's gotta go.

DOUGLAS. *(Rises.)* Of course, you are free to get another opinion. I encourage you to do that — as soon as possible. Then discuss it with your family, or uh, significant, uh ... boyfriend, and ... please ... let me know what you decide. *(There is a pause. Wanda is very frightened.)*

WANDA. No. No … we got a date, doc. *(She leaves, passing Brenda in the hallway.)* Your fucking clinic's not taking anyone new! *(Brenda enters.)*

DOUGLAS. Brenda —

BRENDA. *(Quickly.)* You have several patients —

DOUGLAS. *(Furious.)* Did you tell that woman about Carson? You are not in a position to give medical advice!

BRENDA. Did she say I "advised" her?

DOUGLAS. No, Brenda. And I wouldn't advise anyone else if I were you. Because the clinic's been closed.

BRENDA. What?

DOUGLAS. Contaminated serum. AIDS scare. The FDA —

BRENDA. The FDA can't shut down a Jamaican clinic!

DOUGLAS. The Jamaican government shut it down.

BRENDA. The Jamaicans? *(After a beat.)* Oh, I get it. *(Laughs.)* It was the natives' fault.

DOUGLAS. I'm sure there will be some sort of investigation. *(He rummages for something in his desk.)*

BRENDA. Who will pay for it? The Jamaicans?! *(Wry.)* We just a poor third-world country, Douglas. You're the smart ones.

DOUGLAS. And despite our problems, we have the finest medical system in the world. *(He reaches for Wanda's cigarettes. Brenda grabs them.)*

BRENDA. *(Jamaican intonation.)* Hmmn-hmnn! Got more deaths from smoking than any other "developed" country — but you put a little warning on every pack of cigarettes — and then you go and subsidize your tobacco industry! Why don't your government just shoot you all in the foot? At least it would be something you doctors could fix.

DOUGLAS. Brenda, you are obviously under a lot of stress with school and your job. Maybe you need to take a rest from the books for a while.

BRENDA. I jog for stress.

DOUGLAS. Jog *more.* Now who is waiting out there?

BRENDA. Mrs. From Heaven. Her toe fell off. *(Douglas lights up a cigarette.)*

DOUGLAS. Did she bring it with her?

BRENDA. *(Quietly.)* Maybe you good people just don't want to fix cancer. Maybe there's a cancer industry out there and it does not want to die. After all, no one is in business for their health —

DOUGLAS. *(Voice rising.)* Oh fine. Now we are getting hysterical —
BRENDA.. I am a hysterical woman, Douglas — I'm *stressed!* — forty six thousand women died last year — we don't even put their names on a quilt!
DOUGLAS. Brenda —
BRENDA. I'm scared, Douglas. Every woman in that waiting room — scared to death of her own body!
DOUGLAS. Brenda — I don't know what to tell you! I don't have an answer! *(Beat; explodes.)* IT'S NOT THE DOCTOR'S FAULT! *(Looks at wristwatch; getting hysterical.)* Now, I have an appointment — and I have asked you repeatedly — SEND IN MRS. FROM HEAVEN! GODDAMNIT! DO I HAVE TO GO OUT THERE *MYSELF*?! *(Douglas takes a swipe at his desk. Objects scatter on the floor. He is horrified.)* I'm sorry. I'm sorry. You — you were getting hysterical — I —
BRENDA. I better bring in the next —
DOUGLAS. *(Shaken.)* Brenda ... please ... *(He sinks into the patient's chair, fighting tears.)* There has always been cancer. There was cancer in the bones of dinosaurs. Hippocrates said — when it was deep seated — to just leave it alone. That the patient would live longer that way. And, yes, in two thousand years, when it gets bad, we don't have a whole lot more to offer. I wish to God we did. *(Cries.)* I'm a doctor. I want people to live. But I did not create cancer. And God help me, I cannot cure it either. *(He picks his wife's picture up from the floor.)* Still, I am bound by oath to try. *(Beat; adds quietly.)* And bound by the laws of this country which tell me how I may do so. *(Brenda nods and starts to leave.)* Brenda ... you're going to be a doctor — do you believe in Carson's *theory*?
BRENDA. What — ?
DOUGLAS. That a healthy immune system will destroy its own cancer. Because — if there is something in us — in our *blood* — that can overcome cancer —
BRENDA. You think we goin' overcome *greed*?! Where we goin' catch it? I seen greed in a kiss ... in a billy club ... I seen doctors don't like their patients get too smart. Sure, I think Carson's got a good theory, Douglas. I think Mother Nature has a cure for most everything. *(Pause.)* 'Cept *human* nature ...
DOUGLAS. *(With difficulty.)* Then just bring in the next patient. So I can do the best I can.

BRENDA. *(Checks chart.)* Mrs. From Heaven is waiting. Mrs. Smoot is also waiting. Though I am sure she'd be glad to reschedule. *(They shouldn't, but they exchange a smile.)*
DOUGLAS. Great. Last thing I need right now is to get bit. *(Pause.)* Brenda, I do understand how you feel about Carson.
BRENDA. *(Softly.)* You do? My mother has breast cancer. His serum is saving her life.
DOUGLAS. You never told me.
BRENDA. Hell, everybody's got cancer. Black people just have a little more of it. Just dying a little faster. *(Starts to leave.)* I'll bring in Mrs. From Heaven.
DOUGLAS. Thank you. *(Brenda exits.)* I have an appointment at five. *(After the stage is cleared, Wanda enters in a hospital gown. An Orderly wheels on a gurney, and she gets on. Then Forgiveness and Victoria are wheeled on. There's an odd dance of gurneys ... gurneys moving at angles, or circling slowly, to operating room sounds combined with music that is hauntingly beautiful and disturbing at the same time. As the stage is reset, we should feel as if moving through anesthesia into the next scene.)*

Scene 5

The recovery room.

Victoria is in bed, reading and drinking a Diet Dr. Pepper. The bed is filled with books. She wears her corset open over a Victorian hospital gown, and her flinging-arm-tic has been reduced to a mere flick of the hand. After a moment, Wanda is wheeled in by Nurse Bruce. She is still woozy from anesthesia, and very tired.

NURSE BRUCE. You ring this bell if you need something, girl-friend. *(Wanda nods. Bruce exits.)*
VICTORIA. *(Brightly.)* Hello!
WANDA. *(Weary.)* Oh — hey, how you doin'?
VICTORIA. Oh, fine, fine. I've been here a week, and I'm feeling

almost … chipper! Well, considering my — *(With relish.)* "code-pendency" and my "chronic toxic shame."

WANDA. Oh God.

VICTORIA. My dear — splendid diseases! No surgery, no leeches, no rest cure … Why, even with Freud, one still finds oneself flat on one's back — lying on Freud's filthy couch, Freud thrusting his disgusting theories into one's mind for years and years … *(Picks up a book.)* Now, I've been reading about *Women Who Love Too Much* … and I do seem to have all the classic symptoms, and yet, the odd thing is … *(With difficulty.)* I don't believe I love my husband at all.

WANDA. Sorry. I can't help you. You see … I've never been married at all.

VICTORIA. Ah. Well, then — *(An effort to cheer.) Souvlaki laki verkis!*

WANDA. Thanks. *(Beat.)* What's it mean?

VICTORIA. "The souvlaki is overcooked!" I'm learning Greek! Perhaps we might study together. Or is that "codependent" of me? Tell me, do you think there is such a thing as a "good friend?" Or is a "good friend" just a codependent waiting to be diagnosed? I'd so like to be friends. *(With real concern.)* How are you?

WANDA. I don't know. I guess that's for the doctor to say. They took a — they took my breast.

VICTORIA. That's all?

WANDA. And my tits, of course. *(Beat.)* And they took some lymph nodes to see if they're … "clean."

VICTORIA. Well, I'm sure they're quite clean.

WANDA. So what did they get out of you?

VICTORIA. *(Victorious.) Just* the uterus! I made an agreement with my husband.

WANDA. Oh God.

VICTORIA. You see, the doctor found a small growth which he suspected to be benign, but my husband brought in another physician who thought the uterus to be of no use at all —

WANDA. And you?

VICTORIA. Oh, I agreed absolutely. *(Whispers.)* You see, it turns out I was … with child. I always know right after, ah, conception, because I have a sudden craving for whiskey and cigars.

WANDA. *(Remembers.)* Cigars …

VICTORIA. And since I already have five children I'm not particularly good with — I thought it best to just, ah —

WANDA. Have an abortion. It's okay, I understand.

VICTORIA. An abortion? Good grief, no. A hysterectomy. I'd never have an abortion. It's quite illegal, I'm sure.

WANDA. Well, I've been out for about seven hours — maybe it is now. Okay, gimme the good news.

VICTORIA. *(Delighted.)* I'll be here at least another week. I'm terribly frail. So I'm only allowed visitors every other day! *(Wanda starts to cry.)* I'm sorry. Do you miss your family? Your sweetheart?

WANDA. *(Laughs, cries.)* My tits!

VICTORIA. I see. Sorry … *(Nurse Bruce wheels in a groggy Forgiveness. She wears Chinese pajamas. Her suitcase is on the gurney.)*

NURSE BRUCE. Ring this bell if you need something. *(Forgiveness rings several times.)*

FORGIVENESS. Opium.

NURSE BRUCE. Say what?

FORGIVENESS. Opium!

NURSE BRUCE. *(Coolly.)* I'll get you something for the pain. *(He leaves.)*

Scene 6

The lights fade on the recovery room, and a spot comes up on a phone booth, D.L. Douglas is on the phone.

DOUGLAS. Dr. Saganok, please, Dr. McCaskill calling and no I cannot hold … Good morning, doctor, you have that radiology report for me? … I see. And how was the blood work? … I see. And what is your recommendation? … WHAT?! I'm sorry, doctor, that is not an option … I don't care how many of these cases you've seen. I don't care if you've tried everything, try something else … Well, how about — how about acupuncture? … Look, mister, you don't seem to understand what I'm saying. If it is being tried, I want to try it! I am a doctor — *(Starts to break.)* We don't — just — put our patients to sleep. I — my wife — we — we've had that cat for thirteen years! — she, she's like our — I can't — I just — it would break her heart — it would just shatter her heart in a thousand — ... Don't tell me I'm getting hysterical! I'm a doctor, I can have your goddamn license!... CAN TOO! You're a vet, goddamnit! DO SOMETHING! *(He hangs up, and moves directly into the next scene.)*

Scene 7

Lights up on the recovery room. Victoria's bed is filled with books on cancer. Wanda is reading travel brochures. A popular afternoon talk show is on the TV. A Chinese Intern is making rounds with Douglas, who is trying to examine Forgiveness' foot. She is high, manic.

FORGIVENESS. Oh no, you don't touch golden lotus! You not my husband —
DOUGLAS. *(To Intern.)* We've lost four toes. Gangrene. We're trying to save the foot. Foot binding.
INTERN. Unbelievable. I thought Mao outlawed it in the fifties, so women could work.
DOUGLAS. *(Over-enunciated.)* Please, Mrs. From Heaven, just want to examine — *(Douglas and the Intern try to grab Forgiveness' foot. She keeps kicking them off.)*
FORGIVENESS. *(Laughs.)* Examine? Examine! You want to smell! And lick and bite and suck!
DOUGLAS. No, I assure you —
FORGIVENESS. I'm a married woman! My husband will kill you — you even look at my feet! *(Reaches out to the Intern.)* My husband — my Blessing — ?
INTERN. What should I do, doctor?
DOUGLAS. I — don't know —
FORGIVENESS. Kiss me!
INTERN. Doctor?
DOUGLAS. *(Yells.)* Nurse! *(Forgiveness kicks the Intern.)*
INTERN. Ouch!

FORGIVENESS. Get out of my house! *(Nurse Bruce enters. To Bruce.)* Jade Ornament, show our guests to the door.

DOUGLAS. What the hell is she on?

NURSE BRUCE. Percoset. Anything else she gets from the orderly.

DOUGLAS. *(Gives up.)* I'll check on you tomorrow, Mrs. From Heaven.

FORGIVENESS. *(Charming.)* You call tomorrow. And bring lovely wife.

DOUGLAS. Take care. *(Bruce leaves. To Intern.)* Moving on ... *(They go to Victoria.)* Simple hysterectomy.

INTERN. I see.

VICTORIA. *(Cheerful.)* Good morning, good morning. I love your tie. *(To Intern.)* Yours too.

DOUGLAS. You're looking well, Victoria.

VICTORIA. Yes! *(On second thought.)* Well, not *too* well —

DOUGLAS. I played golf with your husband yesterday.

VICTORIA. *(Covering concern.)* Did you? *(She starts to sneeze ... but doesn't.)*

DOUGLAS. Glad to see that cold's better. We'll have you out of here in no time.

VICTORIA. *(Curses.)* Skata na fas graey thoo rie.

DOUGLAS. Beg your pardon?

VICTORIA. Oh, that's Greek for, "Have you seen my luggage?"

DOUGLAS. I'm glad to see you're keeping a cheerful attitude. You know, I'm reading a remarkable book by a fellow who virtually cured himself of an irreversible disease of the connective tissue by watching —

VICTORIA. French comedies?

DOUGLAS. Yes! I mean, I don't think they were French, but — he did watch comedies. I don't know, maybe he did see a few French ones. *(To Intern.)* You should read this. Have you heard about this?

INTERN. Norman Cousins? I believe he's dead.

DOUGLAS. *(Stricken.)* He is? Oh God. *(Pause; sighs.)* Well. At least he died laughing. *(He begins to crack up, laughing hysterically at his awful joke, the laughter turning to tears. Finally, he feels their eyes on him. Or he gets too close to Forgiveness' foot — and this sobers him. Mortified.)* Sorry. Sorry, bad joke.

VICTORIA. Well, at least you tried. I don't mean to be rude but — I'm doing some research for a friend.

DOUGLAS. I'll give Oliver the good news. *(To Intern.)* Moving on ... *(They start to move to Wanda.)* Why don't you meet me downstairs? *(The Intern nods and leaves. Douglas goes to Wanda. She wears no make-up. Her hair's in a ponytail. He gets her name right.)* How are you, Ms. Kozynski?

WANDA. *(Simply.)* How am I, doctor? *(Douglas sits next to her on the bed.)* Sit down. Make yourself comfortable.

DOUGLAS. Thanks. *(He stretches out his legs on the bed, unconscious of the oddness of the gesture. It looks as if he, too, were a patient.)* Wanda —

WANDA. Uh-oh.

DOUGLAS. The lymph nodes were not what we'd hoped. *(There is a pause.)*

WANDA. I'm sorry they disappointed you. So what do you want to do now? Clean 'em up for me? *(Waits.)* Jees, is the art of conversation dead? Look, just say it, all right? SAY IT!

DOUGLAS. I'm going to have to recommend a rather aggressive course of chemotherapy. I'm sorry.

WANDA. Of course you're sorry. We're all sorry. Stop a stranger on the street and say, "I'm sorry," he'll say, "Oh that's okay." Won't even ask what you're sorry for. Don't be sorry, doc. 'Cause you're not shooting me up with a goddamn thing.

DOUGLAS. I wish I knew another way.

WANDA. You know another way.

DOUGLAS. We've had some very good results.

WANDA. Let's hear the numbers.

DOUGLAS. In cases such as yours ... up to fifty percent cure.

WANDA. *Cure?*

VICTORIA. No recurrence for five years.

WANDA. Five years?

DOUGLAS. That's how we define a cure, yes.

WANDA. I'm going to Jamaica.

DOUGLAS. You can't do that.

FORGIVENESS. *(To Wanda.)* Don't listen. Doctor tell me I got to wear flat shoes. I rather die than wear flat shoes!

WANDA. This is America, doc. Free country.

DOUGLAS. The clinic was permanently closed last week. *(Silence. Then:)*

VICTORIA. There's a clinic in Tijuana using an herbal formula — I read about it in *Mother Jones*. And a clinic in Guadalajara using enzymes —

FORGIVENESS. Actinidia used in China —

VICTORIA. Shark cartilage —

FORGIVENESS. Ginseng —

VICTORIA. Bioelectric therapy — Revici therapy — Burzynski therapy —

FORGIVENESS. Chi gong!

DOUGLAS. Ladies! I — I cannot advise you about these things. They are ... unproven methods.

WANDA. And your methods *are* proven. To suck! *(Starts to cry.)* Sorry. Sorry. I'm in a really bad mood.

DOUGLAS. Here — let me give you a hug. *(He truly tries, but she flings him off.)* Wanda ... There's a study being done on a new drug. Right here in the hospital.

WANDA. What is it?

DOUGLAS. *(With difficulty.)* It's called INT-2.

WANDA. What are the numbers?

DOUGLAS. Well, it hasn't been tested with breast cancer, which is why they're, uh, looking for subjects.

WANDA. How much does it cost to be a guinea pig?

DOUGLAS. If you participate in the trial, your treatment would be free.

WANDA. It would?

DOUGLAS. Of course.

WANDA. So you think I should try it?

DOUGLAS. So far, the work looks ... promising.

WANDA. *(Hopeful like a child.)* So you recommend me trying it?

DOUGLAS. Well — I can't "recommend" it, it's unproven.

WANDA. But in your opinion —

DOUGLAS. Well, I really can't —

WANDA. You're my doctor, damnit!

DOUGLAS. I can't make that decision for you!

WANDA. *(Wildly.)* But you said it was "promising"? I'm not asking you to promise me anything, but you said it was promising? It's promising, right?

DOUGLAS. *(Helplessly.)* Wanda — please. All I can tell you is ... I'm trying it myself. *(The women stare, incredulous. Then Forgiveness climbs out of bed, hobbles over, and gives Douglas a hug, which he returns. Then he lifts her up, carries her back to bed, and leaves. Wanda turns away from the others and pulls the covers over her head.)*

Scene 8

A very hot place. A beach rises up from beneath the stage with Ken and Larry in beach chairs. (This scene is only to be included in a production which can utilize a trap floor. Otherwise, please omit.)

KEN. Do you have any SPF ... *(Looks at sun; worried.)* 30?

LARRY. *(Laughs.)* No, I do not have any SPF 30.

KEN. *("I warned you.")* Okay ... *(Beat.)* Aren't you even a little concerned about exposure?

LARRY. No, Ken, I am not. Nor am I afraid of cigars, electric blankies, the fumes from my 500 SL, or the flesh of things that go "moo." ... See, I'm not the cancer type. I don't hold things inside, like some people. You know — *(Lets it all out.)* Whaaa! *(Laughs.)* I love life, Ken. I just love the fuck out of it.

KEN. Hey, I love life — *(A deep-voiced Jamaican Rasta Waitress enters with drinks.)*

WAITRESS. *(Almost a command.)* You no ready fuh another one?

LARRY. Oh, ya mon. Thanks. *(He holds out his glass. The Waitress pours a concoction that fizzes and smokes. Ken hears her Tourettes-like, added responses, but Larry doesn't.)*

WAITRESS. You welcome. *(Pouring; adds.)* You hairy beached whale, you slimy piece of lard with a credit card.

LARRY. *(Re: drink.)* Thanks, hon. Say, how's the food here?

WAITRESS. Excellent. *(Adds.)* The mayonnaise is bad. And the jerk chicken ain't cooked.

LARRY. Sounds good to me. And would you bring a Mai Tai up to my wife?

WAITRESS. Oh, ya mon. *(Adds.)* She's in the Jacuzzi. With a man with a rash.

LARRY. *(Tucks a bill in the Waitress' skirt.)* Great.

WAITRESS. I saw your black endangered species briefcase in the water, and your Day Planner gettin' nice and wet. Saw your black Guccis, black frame round the picture of your yellow hair sons — I see the black hole where your heart could be. You're

turnin' black, mon. *(To Ken.)* And your drink was FULL of Sweet'N Low. *(Ken gasps.)*
LARRY. You know, you look familiar, hon?
WAITRESS. Ya, man. I-man everywhere. *(Laughs.)* And you know I and I all look the same. *(Leaving.)* Cool runnings! *(As she exits, the sun gets redder, the reggae more discordant. Ken is really scared.)*
KEN. Boy, it's really hot.
LARRY. *(Loves it.)* Mmmmnnn.
KEN. Don't you feel it?
LARRY. Nope. I don't, Ken. I don't feel a thing. *(The beach starts to sink down under, as the slowed reggae dissolves into the sound of a popular late-night talk show.)*

Scene 9

Night. Victoria can't concentrate on her book. Wanda looks a mess. She's eating junk food, crumpling wrappers. Forgiveness is watching a late-night talk show. Finally, Victoria can't stand it anymore and goes to Wanda.

VICTORIA. My good woman. You can't just lie there partaking of Ding Dong after Ding Dong. Are you going to try the new treatment or not? *(Wanda mumbles, munching, "don't know.")* Skata.
FORGIVENESS. *(Yells at the TV.)* Stupid pet tricks! I want to see stupid pet tricks! Stupid pet tricks right now or I break your face!
VICTORIA. Mrs. From Heaven, please.
FORGIVENESS. He knows I like the stupid pet tricks. That's why he won't do them no more. He's a *bad* man! Keeps the stupid pets locked away with chains on their stupid feet so they can't get out of the television! Even the kitten cats. Cats good luck! Good luck! *(To the TV.)* Meow! Meeeeow! I scratch your eyes out, motherfucker!
VICTORIA. *(Calls offstage.)* Nurse Bruce! *(Nurse Bruce enters.)*
NURSE BRUCE. Whaddup?
VICTORIA. *(Indicates Forgiveness.)* If you please. *(Bruce prepares a shot for Forgiveness, as Victoria searches for a book.)*
FORGIVENESS. Meoooow!

NURSE BRUCE. *(Pets Forgiveness.)* All right, baby. Chill. *(He gives her a shot and she lies back. Her theme begins, as Blessing enters in her dream with a tray of tea. Two scenes play independently. Wanda, in the middle, keeps eating.)*

VICTORIA. Bruce, while you were making up the bedsheets this morning, did you happen to find —

NURSE BRUCE. Say *what?*

VICTORIA. I said, did you happen to find my copy of Dr. Wilhelm Reich's *The Function of the Orgasm*? It was right here in my pillow sham.

BLESSING. First wife ...

NURSE BRUCE. Do I go in your pillow sham? *(He plumps Victoria's pillows, giving one a good punch.)*

BLESSING. I have brought tea. *(He serves them.)*

WANDA. Yo, Bruce, something for the pain?

NURSE BRUCE. Hold on, baby. *(Blessing starts to make love to Forgiveness.)*

BLESSING. I have missed you.

FORGIVENESS. My Blessing ...

VICTORIA. Nurse Bruce, I may be leaving soon. I want *The Function of the Orgasm*! And I want it right now!

FORGIVENESS. Yes!

NURSE BRUCE. *(Taps name tag.)* You see this? It says RN, baby. I ain't your fucking maid. Dig?

BLESSING. First Wife. Forgive me. I must go! *(As he leaves, he crosses Bruce.)*

FORGIVENESS. My husband — my Blessing!

NURSE BRUCE. Do I look like your husband? *(Leaves, muttering.)* Five wives, shit. Some men just don't know when to stop. *(He exits.)*

FORGIVENESS. No! Noooo!

WANDA. NURSE, GODDAMNIT! I'm supposed to be comfortable. I'm not —

VICTORIA. Shut up! Both of you! I mean — *(Thinks; decides.)* Do shut up. *(Victoria goes to Wanda's bed, clears the Ding Dong wrappers, and takes her by the shoulders.)* There now. Are you going to try the new treatment?

WANDA. Don't know. It's an "unproven method."

VICTORIA. Then will you do as the doctor earlier prescribed?

WANDA. *(Shrugs; wry.)* All my life I let guys do pretty much what they wanted with my body ... *(Victoria goes back to her own bed.)*

FORGIVENESS. Got to be First Wife! Not Fifth Wife! How you going to eat? Who going to take care of you?

WANDA. *(Simply.)* I really don't know.

VICTORIA. My dear, you have the vote, you can learn Greek, you have no obligations, you can read any book in the world — if you don't have a goddamn answer, who does?

WANDA. Hey, I'm *thinking*, all right? It takes longer. *(She swallows one last bite.)* Look. My whole family got ... *(It's the first time she's said the word.)* cancer. *(Touches her breast.)* My grandmother ... *(Touches her stomach.)* my grandfather ... *(Touches her breast.)* my aunt ... *(Touches her groin.)* my uncle ... *(Hits her head.)* his wife ... *(Brenda enters, U., in street clothes, carrying a suitcase. She waits, not wanting to interrupt.)* My mom never even lived to win the stupid bet. My dad never got to see me ... pretty. *(Forces a smile.)* Well, hey, I wouldn't want him to see me like this now would I? And, you know, Vic, I got a girlfriend — they took a lump, they gave her chemo, and she's just fine. She's fine! Well, her hair fell out, and she went through menopause at thirty-six, and her boyfriend left her for the radiologist ... But she's fine. But I don't have a little lump of cancer. I'm a big girl, I got a lot of it. The hospital says my insurance won't kick in for *six* months now, at which point I may not be around to enjoy my benefits — which may all be beside the point anyway, because this morning I called my job and I'm fired.

VICTORIA. Oh dear. *(Brenda goes to Wanda.)*

BRENDA. I hear they have a bed waiting for you upstairs, chile.

WANDA. Hey — come on in! Have a Ding Dong, they took our cigars.

BRENDA. Don't eat nuh sugar.

WANDA. You got a suitcase —

BRENDA. Me No Send, You No Come ...

WANDA. *(To Victoria.)* You know, maybe I'll see Tijuana, or Guadalajara —

FORGIVENESS. But doctor say —

WANDA. *(Explodes.)* I KNOW! I know what the doctor said!

FORGIVENESS. No need to speak loudly.

WANDA. Forgive me. But this cancer ... it's in *my* body. It's not in your body — *(To Victoria.)* or your body, or the good doctor's body — I know he's got his cancer, but this cancer is ... mine. For better or worse, till death do us part, it's about the one thing I got left that's all — mine. And if I want to take it to Tijuana or

Guadafuckinglajara — I've never been out of the tri-state area! *(Fights tears.)* If I want to die. If I want to call up my doctor and say, "No thank you very much," or "Please, God, help me!" — for once in my lousy screwed up life, it's MY BODY! MY BODY! MINE! *(Pause; laughs.)* And you know what I figured out this morning?

BRENDA. *(Gently.)* What?

VICTORIA. Frankly, you baffle me —

WANDA. I sat down with a pencil and paper and figured out I've spend 6,750 hours of my life ... on my hair. Nine months washing off my waterproof mascara.

FORGIVENESS. Mascara?

WANDA. You don't wanna know. So, with all the time I'm going to save from now on, going around looking like shit ... what if I take a *little* time — and make up my mind about my body. I mean, for chrissakes, I'm only forty —

VICTORIA. *(Shocked.)* Forty?!

BRENDA. *(Smiles.)* Go chile.

WANDA. And, yeah, dying would be a bitch. But isn't it worse — not living while you're alive?

BRENDA. You're doin' all right, Ms. Kozynski. Whatever you decide. *(She gives Wanda a hug — which she accepts.)*

VICTORIA. *(Warmly.)* And of course I understand the *theory* of what you're saying. I'm not sure I understand precisely what you mean by the word ... "living"? *(The women look out, thinking, as the light starts to change. During the light change that takes us into the next scene, Brenda is replaced by Oliver.)*

Scene 10

Victoria is still looking out, thinking.

OLIVER. Sweetums — *(Victoria is startled, but does not turn.)*

VICTORIA. How are you, Oliver?

FORGIVENESS. *(Stoned.)* Hey, sailor —

VICTORIA. This is Forgiveness.

OLIVER. How do you do?

FORGIVENESS. Oh, fine.

OLIVER. *(Overlapping, to Victoria.)* I'm fine.

VICTORIA. And this is Wanda —

OLIVER. Ah yes, the lady with the ah —

FORGIVENESS. Everybody fine! *(She turns on the TV. A jolly family sitcom plays in the background.)*

VICTORIA. And the ... children?

OLIVER. Felicity is at the zoo. With Bridget. She'd like very much for you to come home, Victoria. As would your other children. *(Pause.)* As would I. *(Forgiveness laughs at the TV.)*

VICTORIA. I'm ... not well, Oliver.

OLIVER. The doctor says you are fine, love. I'll take care of you — *(Victoria sneezes.)* Poor sweetums. Felicity has a cold too. *(Victoria reacts.)*

VICTORIA. Felicity ... is sneezing now?

OLIVER. Just a cold, love. I'm sure once you're home, she'll be fine. I have a touch of the flu myself. *(He feels his forehead.)*

WANDA. Maybe you shouldn't get too close. Germs and all.

OLIVER. I am a doctor, madam.

WANDA. I know. *(Oliver scowls at her and goes to Victoria.)*

OLIVER. Shall I pack for you, sweetums? *(Forgiveness laughs at the TV. Victoria points to her books, a challenge.)*

VICTORIA. I'd ... be taking these, Oliver.

OLIVER. Yes? Very good then. *(Beat.)* All of them, love?

VICTORIA. All of them.

WANDA. *(Holds out magazines.)* Don't forget these. *(Oliver reluctantly takes the* Cosmopolitan *and starts to gather books.)*

OLIVER. *(Sotto; to Victoria.)* I, ah — read the Freud, love.

VICTORIA. Yes?

OLIVER. Indeed, love, I concede I ... have a problem.

VICTORIA. *(Hopeful.)* Yes?

OLIVER. My mother. My mu — mu — mummy was a charming — well-traveled — *(Breaks.)* — castrating bi — *(Wanda and Forgiveness stare.)*

VICTORIA. *(Quickly.)* Would you wait outside, Oliver, while I change?

OLIVER. *(Recovers.)* Of course. I'll be downstairs in the carriage. *(He kisses her, gratefully, and leaves. Victoria's theme begins. She closes her corset, and, with great dignity, begins to dress in her twenty pounds of clothes.)*

WANDA. You sure you're ready to leave?

VICTORIA. I have to.

WANDA. You don't have to.

VICTORIA. Yes. I do.

FORGIVENESS. Tell him to get other wives.

VICTORIA. I can't.

FORGIVENESS. Then tell him go fuck himself.

VICTORIA. I can't. My husband ... needs me. And my daughter — *(Fighting tears.)* My daughter ... has a cold. *(Victoria exchanges a look with Wanda, who understands.)*

WANDA. I'd like to give you something.

VICTORIA. No, please — *(Wanda hands her a jar filled with a bluish fluid and her "tits.")*

WANDA. Here. To remember me by.

VICTORIA. But we'll see each other in the waiting room, won't we? And it's always such a long wait, isn't it?

WANDA. *(Sighs.)* It's a long wait. Yeah.

VICTORIA. Wait for me ... *(She holds out her hand, and they hold tight. Then Victoria turns, kisses Forgiveness and leaves. Forgiveness laughs at the TV. In the scene change, Douglas enters with the Orderly and they remove Victoria's bed. Brenda enters and crosses the periphery of the stage with a suitcase, as if checking on her patients one last time. Douglas and Brenda have a moment of understanding and acknowledgment. Then they go off in opposite directions. The Orderly hands Forgiveness a joint and leaves too.)*

Scene 11

As the lights change, Wanda is reading Forgiveness a bedtime story. Forgiveness is smoking a joint.

WANDA. ... But Snow White's wicked old step-mother was also bidden to the wedding feast, and when she went to the mirror and said, "Mirror mirror on the wall, who is the fairest of us all?" the mirror answered, "O Queen, although you are of beauty rare, the young bride is a thousand times more fair." And when the old

Queen saw Snow White, she could not stir from the place for terror. And they had red hot iron shoes ready for her, in which the old Queen had to dance and dance until she fell down dead. *(Pause.)* And Snow White and the prince lived happily ever after."

FORGIVENESS. Good story.

WANDA. Uh-huh. *(Thinks.)* If you're young and beautiful, some old broad's gonna try to knock you off. And if you're ugly or old, you're screwed. *(Tosses book.)* These Grimm boys got you coming and going.

FORGIVENESS. One more story, mother. Can't sleep — my feet are on fire!

WANDA. Your turn.

FORGIVENESS. Okay ... *(Takes a drag.)* Once upon a time, in the Flowery Kingdom, there lived an Empress named Tu Chin. And her feet were twelve inches big.

WANDA. No kidding?

FORGIVENESS. And everybody told the Emperor, what a lucky man you are to have a wife with such big beautiful feet. Only problem was, the Empress — she walked in her sleep. So the Emperor had eight inches cut off, so she couldn't roam around in the night and embarrass him. And the Empress felt so bad, so ugly. And, because the Emperor loved her so much, he made all the other ladies of the Flowery Kingdom cut their feet real small, so the Empress would not die of humiliation. And from then on, all the little girls in the Flowery Kingdom were bound.

WANDA. *(After a moment.)* Where's the happy ending?

FORGIVENESS. Chinese story. Happy ending not necessary. Maybe happy ending in next life. Tell another, mother.

WANDA. Turn on *The Tonight Show.*

FORGIVENESS. Just one more ... *(Wanda starts to reach for the book of fairy tales, but changes her mind and starts to make up her own.)*

WANDA. Okay. Once upon a time there were three sisters. All of them stupid. One thought her feet were too big, one thought her waist was too big, and the really stupid one thought her tits weren't big *enough.* So they went to a Magician and said, "Make us perfect." And he held up a magic mirror which made the sisters look like —

FORGIVENESS. Woman in Taurus commercial.

WANDA. Okay. And the Magician said, "You too can look just like this." And the sisters gave him a pile of gold, and the Magician worked his magic ... and built a new tennis court with their money. But, after a few years, the magic started to ... go bad.

FORGIVENESS. *(Softly.)* Sisters not lucky.

WANDA. No. And the sisters went back to the Magician and he said, "Hey, I said I'd make you perfect. I didn't say you'd be perfect *forever.* Check out the shingle. It says, 'Magician,' not 'God.'" And the sisters were really pissed off. So what did they do?

FORGIVENESS. Wait for luck to change ... *(She closes her eyes and nods every once in a while at the story.)*

WANDA. First, they took all the mirrors in the kingdom and smashed 'em ... and recycled the glass. Then they told all their girl-friends and daughters, "Next time you want to look in a mirror, don't go to the Magician, come to us." And when the women came to check out their thighs and their noses and all their other problems, they had to look in the sisters' eyes. And the sisters would say, "Oh, gimme a break, you look fine." At first the women didn't believe them, 'cause who believes you when you tell 'em they look good, right? But the sisters kept saying, "You're beautiful."

FORGIVENESS. Beautiful ... *(Forgiveness smiles and lies perfectly still. Wanda continues, unaware.)*

WANDA. And eventually the women started to buy it. And the Magicians were doing such lousy business, they all had to move to ... Europe. It was like magic. Everybody got kissed, and the women who felt like it got married. And the ones who didn't got good jobs in the kingdom. *(Realizes.)* And some got both! And everybody lived a whole lot happier ever after. *(She turns to Forgiveness.)* Forgiveness? *(Waits; cries.)* Forgiveness?! *(She understands that Forgiveness is gone.)* Good night, Forgiveness From Heaven. Sweet dreams. *(Wanda turns out the light next to her bed. After a moment, a white spot comes up over Forgiveness. Slowly, she sits up into the light. Then she stands up on the bed and has a good stretch. Joyful Chinese music begins. Forgiveness jumps down and starts to unwrap her feet, as if unwrapping the bound years ... first with the relief of the aging woman, then faster, with the joy of the bound five-year-old child. She begins to dance an ancient Chinese ribbon dance with her bindings. She dances and dances, spinning off the yoke of the centuries ... And the light fades on her dancing.)*

End of Play

PROPERTY LIST

ACT ONE

Vogue magazine (FORGIVENESS)
Cosmopolitan magazine (VICTORIA)
Pack of cigarettes (WANDA)
Purse (WANDA)
Paper with pencil or pen (BRENDA)
Medical chart (DOUGLAS)
Duster (BRIDGET)
Cigar and matches (OLIVER)
Golf clubs and balls (DOUGLAS)
Antique golf clubs and balls (OLIVER)
Cellular phone (LARRY)
Watch (OLIVER)
3 glasses of water (ATTENDANT)
1 Tylenol tablet (ATTENDANT)
Inhaler (KEN)
Chopsticks (BLESSING)
Bowl of leeches (JADE ORNAMENT)
Teapot (FORGIVENESS)
Opium pipe (JADE ORNAMENT, FORGIVENESS)
Shots of vodka (WOMAN LAWYER)
The New York Times (WOMAN LAWYER)
Lighter or matches (WANDA)
Keys (KEN)
Beer (WAITRESS)
Books (BRENDA)
Briefcase (WOMAN LAWYER)
Cup (BRENDA)
Book on Freud (VICTORIA)
Cigars (VICTORIA)
Suitcase (FORGIVENESS, NURSE BRUCE)
Pill (LARRY)
Cane (FORGIVENESS, NURSE BRUCE)
Cigars and lighter or matches (VICTORIA)

Glamour magazine (WANDA)
List of books (VICTORIA)
Purse (VICTORIA)
Romance novel (VICTORIA)
Large round Chinese basket (FORGIVENESS)
Leaves (FORGIVENESS)
Pill (LARRY)
2 glasses of water (CERISE)
Appointment chart (BRENDA)
Wristwatch (DOUGLAS)
Picture of Judy (DOUGLAS)
Diet Dr. Pepper (VICTORIA)
Books (VICTORIA)
Travel brochures (WANDA)
Drinks (WAITRESS)
Drinking glass (LARRY)
Bill (money) (LARRY)
Needle (NURSE BRUCE)
Tray of tea (BLESSING)
Name tag (NURSE BRUCE)
Ding Dongs and wrappers (WANDA)
Suitcase (BRENDA)
Magazines (WANDA)
Jar with fluid and tit (WANDA)
Joint (ORDERLY)
Book of fairy tales (WANDA)
Foot bindings (FORGIVENESS)

SOUND EFFECTS

Birds
Traffic sounds
Rap music
New-age music
Operating room sounds
Reggae music

NEW PLAYS

★ **AGES OF THE MOON by Sam Shepard.** Byron and Ames are old friends, reunited by mutual desperation. Over bourbon on ice, they sit, reflect and bicker until fifty years of love, friendship and rivalry are put to the test at the barrel of a gun. "A poignant and honest continuation of themes that have always been present in the work of one of this country's most important dramatists, here reconsidered in the light and shadow of time passed." –NY Times. "Finely wrought...as enjoyable and enlightening as a night spent stargazing." –Talkin' Broadway. [2M] ISBN: 978-0-8222-2462-4

★ **ALL THE WAY by Robert Schenkkan. Winner of the 2014 Tony Award for Best Play.** November, 1963. An assassin's bullet catapults Lyndon Baines Johnson into the presidency. A Shakespearean figure of towering ambition and appetite, this charismatic, conflicted Texan hurls himself into the passage of the Civil Rights Act—a tinderbox issue emblematic of a divided America—even as he campaigns for re-election in his own right, and the recognition he so desperately wants. In Pulitzer Prize and Tony Award–winning Robert Schenkkan's vivid dramatization of LBJ's first year in office, means versus ends plays out on the precipice of modern America. ALL THE WAY is a searing, enthralling exploration of the morality of power. It's not personal, it's just politics. "...action-packed, thoroughly gripping... jaw-dropping political drama." –Variety. "A theatrical coup...nonstop action. The suspense of a first-class thriller." –NY1. [17M, 3W] ISBN: 978-0-8222-3181-3

★ **CHOIR BOY by Tarell Alvin McCraney.** The Charles R. Drew Prep School for Boys is dedicated to the creation of strong, ethical black men. Pharus wants nothing more than to take his rightful place as leader of the school's legendary gospel choir. Can he find his way inside the hallowed halls of this institution if he sings in his own key? "[An] affecting and honest portrait...of a gay youth tentatively beginning to find the courage to let the truth about himself become known." –NY Times. "In his stirring and stylishly told drama, Tarell Alvin McCraney cannily explores race and sexuality and the graces and gravity of history." –NY Daily News. [7M] ISBN: 978-0-8222-3116-5

★ **THE ELECTRIC BABY by Stefanie Zadravec.** When Helen causes a car accident that kills a young man, a group of fractured souls cross paths and connect around a mysterious dying baby who glows like the moon. Folk tales and folklore weave throughout this magical story of sad endings, strange beginnings and the unlikely people that get you from one place to the next. "The imperceptible magic that pervades human existence and the power of myth to assuage sorrow are invoked by the playwright as she entwines the lives of strangers in THE ELECTRIC BABY, a touching drama." –NY Times. "As dazzling as the dialogue is dreamful." –Pittsburgh City Paper. [3M, 3W] ISBN: 978-0-8222-3011-3

DRAMATISTS PLAY SERVICE, INC.
440 Park Avenue South, New York, NY 10016 212-683-8960 Fax 212-213-1539
postmaster@dramatists.com www.dramatists.com